A CURLEW
IN THE
FOREGROUND

An RSPB warden's summer on North Uist

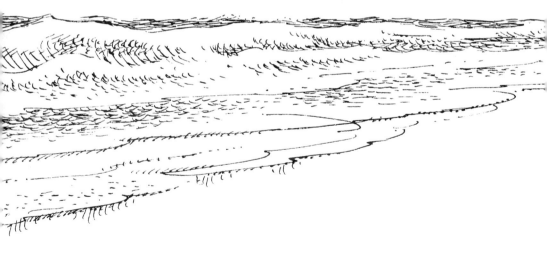

A CURLEW
IN THE
FOREGROUND

Philip Coxon

DAVID & CHARLES

Newton Abbot   London   North Pomfret (Vt)

For Eileen

British Library Cataloguing in Publication Data

Coxon, Philip
   A curlew in the foreground.
   1. North Uist——Description and travel
   I. Title
   914.11'4   DA880.N6

   ISBN 0-7153-9103-8

Line illustrations by John Paley
Maps by Ethan Danielson

© Text: Philip Coxon 1988

Typeset by ABM Typographics Limited Hull
Printed in Great Britain
by Butler & Tanner Limited, Frome and London
for David & Charles Publishers plc
Brunel House   Newton Abbot   Devon

Published in the United States of America
by David & Charles Inc
North Pomfret   Vermont 05053   USA

PREFACE

This lyrical book was written by a man whose life was inspired by a love of wild birds and wild places. It was in Wales that I first met Philip Coxon – for a time he was my assistant when I was warden of the Ynys-hir reserve of the Royal Society for the Protection of Birds. It was from Ynys-hir that he was sent by the RSPB to look after their beautiful, bird-rich Balranald reserve in the Outer Hebrides, and this was just the experience that he needed. For it is a place of lonely marshes, desolate shores and often angry seas, raging winds and driving rain. It is also the home of crofters whose way of life, happily for nature conservation, has not kept pace with that of the mainland. There he spent a rewarding, sometimes idyllic, sometimes difficult, spring and summer, recording the natural scene and helping many a visiting birdwatcher to see the birds without disturbing them.

There was, however, more to Philip Coxon than a skilful naturalist. He also had a very observant eye for people, especially the various members of the crofting community of which for the time being he found himself a part. But what singles him out most of all is that he was a born writer and there in North Uist he found a wonderful theme. His word pictures of the birds and their distinctive habitats are delightfully vivid and so are the intimate sketches of his crofter neighbours. His burning private ambition was to be a novelist (Henry Williamson was his literary hero) and hence the strong story line that runs through his book. It is tragic that so promising a writer died so young. But we can be thankful that he managed to complete a book that is so clearly in the best tradition of English nature writing.

William Condry

INTRODUCTION

During the winter of 1973–4, I worked for the Royal Society for the Protection of Birds as assistant warden of their reserve at Ynys-hir, on the Dovey estuary in Wales. Although most of my life until then had been in Scotland and my first love was for the Highlands, I came to have a high regard for Ynys-hir. I liked the variety of landscape and habitat packed into its 650 acres; positioned at the head of the estuary, it included tidal mud-flats and salt-marshes, freshwater bog, farmland, deciduous and coniferous woodland and part of a steep rocky hillside to the south of the estuary.

In Scotland, and through previous experience with the RSPB on a reserve in mid-Wales, I had developed an affinity for uplands. I liked a fair proportion of vertical in my landscape, preferred the quiet and withdrawn atmosphere of mountain country. Before the Ynys-hir experience I related the coast of England and Wales with seaside: crowded, spoiled by tourism, often industrial development and housing. The coast of north-west Scotland was unspoiled – but then, it was all part of mountain landscape; south of the border, the coast was only for families of trippers with small children.

Ynys-hir, then, was a revelation. The estuary fascinated me, the bare levels of sand-bars and mud-flats which looked simple from a distance but were in fact complicated by a maze of creeks and channels, divided into different textures of sand and mud, changing all the time according to condition of tide and weather. The salt-marshes also had a spacious quality, but were broken into areas of sward, spartina and other rushes and reeds, all deeply dissected by creeks which coiled about in all directions, some firm enough to walk, others dangerously soft. I had to learn this habitat; where to go safely at all states of tide, how to make use of creeks and taller vegetation when attempting to approach birds. It was abundant in its wildlife as no other habitat, and I also became addicted to the

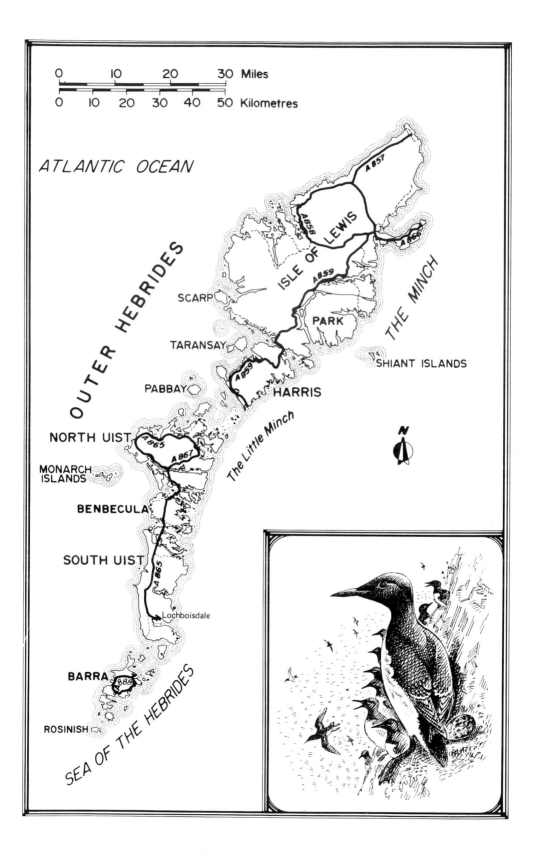

0   10   20   30 Miles

0   10   20   30   40   50 Kilometres

ATLANTIC OCEAN

OUTER HEBRIDES

ISLE OF LEWIS

A 857

A 858

A 859

THE MINCH

SCARP

PARK

TARANSAY

SHIANT ISLANDS

PABBAY

A 859

HARRIS

NORTH UIST

A 865

A 867

The Little Minch

MONARCH
ISLANDS

BENBECULA

SOUTH UIST

A 865

Lochboisdale

BARRA

A 888

SEA OF THE HEBRIDES

ROSINISH

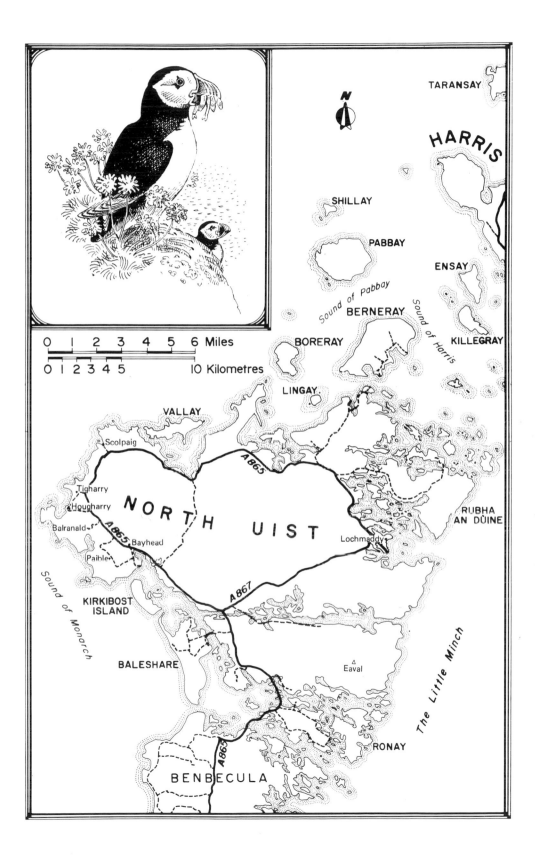

TARANSAY

HARRIS

SHILLAY

PABBAY

ENSAY

Sound of Pabbay

BERNERAY

KILLEGRAY

BORERAY

Sound of Harris

LINGAY

VALLAY

A863

RUBHA
AN DÚINE

Scolpaig

N O R T H   U I S T

Tigharry

Hougharry

Balranald

A865

Bayhead

Lochmaddy

Paible

A867

KIRKIBOST
ISLAND

Sound of Monarch

The Little Minch

BALESHARE

Eaval

RONAY

A865

B E N B E C U L A

| 0 | 1 | 2 | 3 | 4 | 5 | 6 Miles |

| 0 | 1 | 2 | 3 | 4 | 5 | 10 Kilometres |

aesthetic quality of estuaries, a different sort of desolation from that offered by mountains, but if anything even more compelling.

Inevitably, I became involved with the work of the reserve and the RSPB's plans to improve it both as wildlife habitat and for the enjoyment and edification of visitors. The head warden was in the process of drawing up the first management plans and he allowed me to study this document. There were plans for improving the woodlands by cutting out rhododendron and allowing the re-growth of indigenous scrub and trees, and encouraging more natural gradation of wood to open field by introducing a zone of intermediate habitat. Instead of standing tall and distinct, the woods should grade softly through thorn scrub and sapling to stands of reed and rush and finally to a grassland which near the estuary was naturally marshy, with many open pools.

In another part of the reserve, a chain of freshwater meres was to be excavated behind one of the sea walls and diversified by the construction of islands in the meres and a programme of tree planting on the banks. Plans were made for hides to be built in the woods overlooking the meres and approaches devised so that birdwatchers should be able to enjoy the area without disturbing what they had come to see.

This management plan seemed admirable. Reading it and imagining what Ynys-hir might become if its proposals were implemented helped me to identify with the reserve and its future.

I might not be able, however, to stay at Ynys-hir to see the management plan put into operation. It was RSPB policy to move young single wardens like myself from reserve to reserve, giving us a variety of experience before taking charge of a reserve of our own. A single season was all that we might reasonably expect in any one place and we knew that in summer we might be sent out to take charge of any one of a number of reserves wardened only between April and September each year. Many of these 'summer reserves' were in remote parts of Britain, places where birdwatching visitors did not venture in winter.

My moving orders arrived one wet day in February. Sitting on the floor of the warden's office, we were both working absorbedly on maps to go with the management plan. The warden's wife had been up to the post-box at the main road a mile away and among all the bulky daily mail to the reserve was one slim vital envelope from the society's headquarters to me.

It instructed me to prepare myself to take charge of the RSPB's reserve at Balranald, on the island of North Uist in the Outer Hebrides, not later than 20 March of that year. I should contact the society's Scottish office in Edinburgh immediately and arrange to call there for a briefing on my way from Ynys-hir to Balranald.

My first reaction was one of angry disappointment. It wasn't fair, to be encouraged to identify with Ynys-hir and all its problems, then moved after only one winter season to the other end of Britain.

But the warden wouldn't allow me to indulge in depression. He was sorry to lose me, but then I should be grateful for the chance of taking full responsibility for a reserve. Assistant wardenship had its limitations; surely it was more interesting to make and follow my own management plan rather than merely help with someone else's. It was true that I could do nothing at Ynys-hir which any other assistant could not. To express individual convictions about reserve management would require full control of a site.

The warden's wife, still in rain-splashed wellingtons and water-proofs, pulled a road map of northern Britain from the office shelf. We traced the route across all Wales, half of England to Scotland and Edinburgh, then diagonally across Scotland to the romantic west and the island of Skye. Some 30 miles west of Skye were the Outer Hebrides, like a string of floating beads. North Uist was one of the smaller beads, second from the north after Harris and Lewis.

'What an adventure,' said the warden's wife.

During the following weeks, maps of my new reserve began to arrive from the society's HQ in Bedfordshire. Balranald occupied the extreme north-western corner of North Uist, including a head-land which seemed ready to break off into the open Atlantic and a tiny island called Causamul, 3 miles off-shore. Most of the reserve's 1,500 acres seemed to be crofting land, divided between two main coastal townships, Hougharry in the north, Balranald a mile or two further south. Maps at 1in scale enabled me to relate North Uist to the western Highland mainland and other islands in the Outer Hebrides. At 6in scale, I could compare the reserve to the rest of North Uist and at 25in to the mile, see details of the reserve itself.

Already familiar with much of the western Highland mainland

Herons

and Skye, now I had to consider crossing that known territory, loved for its mountains, and continue westwards oversea for the relatively low-lying outer isles. On the smaller-scale maps were splotches of brown, indicating upland on Harris and South Uist; but between the more mountainous islands, North Uist and Benbecula sat round and green like a couple of grassy pancakes and their main feature was not upland but rather the amount of water they included in the way of lochs and inlets. A large-scale map told me that the reserve itself was a flat and watery place. It edged the Atlantic on three sides with a succession of beaches and low headlands and to the east petered out indefinitely towards a boggy moor. The middle of the reserve area also had open water – a large shallow loch, surrounded on the map by those tufty eyebrow symbols indicating marshland. Between these natural features and the scattered houses of the townships stretched something called machair, about which nothing could be deduced from the maps except that it was extremely flat. The highest point on the whole reserve was a knoll in the south-western corner reaching the most un-Highland eminence of 30ft.

This was altogether a flatter, wetter and in places more densely populated region than anywhere in the Highlands, and, despite the maps, no clear image was formed in my mind of what it was really like. It was good for birds; the rest was all mysterious as a Celtic twilight. I would have to wait and see; but as February passed into March I was increasingly eager to be off.

The last few days of my term at Ynys-hir were spent in the spirit of half nostalgia, half keen anticipation. We did some work on the sluices for the projected meres and my last job was to plant out a hundred sapling Scots pine trees among clumps of ancient pines which supported a heronry. Both trees and birds figure in the folklore of the area and in planting replacement pines I was helping to perpetuate wildlife and human cultural tradition. It was a lovely place to work, by the estuary with its flighting wildfowl and advancing or retreating tides. I lingered over the job, settling each tree carefully into the rocky soil, spreading the roots to give maximum freedom, scooping back soil against rabbits with a cylinder of chicken wire, and each was stroked and given my blessing before passing on to the next. Around me in the salt-marsh pools and

13

above me in the old trees, herons were already gathering to begin their breeding season.

I arranged to leave Ynys-hir early one Monday morning and went down to the warden's home on the Sunday evening to say my farewells. They were selfless, dedicated people, the warden and his wife; they taught me much about conservation and wildlife, and they had shown me a great deal of simple human kindness. I left them sadly and late, but instead of taking the farm track directly to my own cottage, branched off on a side track through the woods. It was a bright moonlit night; I found my way easily through oaks and shadows to a ridge and a clearing which overlooked the whole length of the Dovey estuary. There it was outspread in the moon-light. The tide was at extreme ebb, sands and creeks exposed to the night sky. Out there I could hear but not see thousands of shore birds: waders with clear or shrill calls, a mixed gabbling and whistling of many ducks, and occasionally the deeper calls of geese and wild swans.

Below me in the woods owls were hooting and a fox barked from the flat marshy fields between woodland and shore. Night and the estuary were intensely alive. Humanity, as represented by lights from Aberdovey across the sands and a scatter of twinklings from farmhouses under the hills, for once seemed to fit harmoniously into the whole. Superbly situated among the last grouping of trees above the salt-marshes, a light from the warden's house shone through winter branches. Estuary, hills, wildlife and friendship: I wondered doubtfully whether Uist could offer as much.

A CURLEW IN THE FOREGROUND

Corn bunting

North Uist is a roughly circular island of about 15 miles diameter and is served by a road which follows the coast. A car ferry operates between Uig in Skye and Lochmaddy. Lochmaddy, the island's port and only town, is in the south-east. My destination was a croft called The Glebe, near the township of Hougharry in the extreme north-west. The map indicated an obvious route leaving Lochmaddy and turning west for 12 miles to the west coast, then turning north. Six miles up the west coast is the township of Bayhead, second in size of the North Uist settlements; and 4 miles north of Bayhead, the turning to The Glebe was on my right. All very simple, and if I lost my way towards the end of my journey, I would only have to ask anyone for The Glebe's owner, a Mr Murdo Macdonald.

The sheer unfamiliarity of the terrain was confusing. No map could give a true impression of this landscape. For one thing, the broad red line indicating the 'A' class trunk road on the map and travelling reasonably directly, was in fact a tortuous little single track which twisted around loch sides and bog hollows and defied all sense of direction. The landscape seen by van headlights was alarming: so much water, sometimes on each side of the road, that I might still be travelling by ferry. Between areas of water were strips of heather and moor grasses shrunken by strong wind and onto everything rain poured down.

Not surprisingly in this inhospitable landscape, there was no settlement once Lochmaddy was passed. It was a world inhabited only by wind and rain. There seemed no alternative but to follow the road wherever it was going, so I drove slowly for what seemed a long way over this island, mile after mile of watery nightmare.

Settlement was reached again at the island's west coast and there was immediate change from uninhabited watery moorland to croft-land with many houses. At the roadside now were wire fences, wintry grasses and areas of reeds and rush. I turned north into an even stronger wind, and after a mile or two of confident driving began to be bewildered again. According to the map a couple of minor townships occurred before Bayhead. But there were houses all the way on each side of the road, like one continuous township. Any of the houses on the right might be The Glebe, with a family inside anxiously waiting for me to appear.

Nothing for it but to stop and ask the way of someone. I saw a house near the road and parked on the track leading up to it. Battling with the van door to open it against the wind, I was immediately aware of that smell which was to become so familiar. A compound of seaweed and rain and peat-smoke, acid and invigorating and mixed with the universal hill-farm smell of sheep. I fumbled with the wire and string which fastened the gate, then clambered over and fought my way up the path to the house. One window showed light dimly behind a heavy curtain. A dog in an outhouse began to bark ferociously. Had the animal been free, my welcome to Uist would have been a thorough mauling. The door of the house was opened slightly and someone called out in Gaelic. A curse for me or a greeting, or a rebuke for the barking dog? I answered in my English and the door opened widely. A mild-faced, silvery-haired old man stood there, shepherd's crook in one hand, the other hand holding the door steady against the wind. You have to step into a house in Uist, the wind won't let you introduce yourself over the doorstep. In the half-lit hallway I shook rain off my coat and apologised for the intrusion. The question, softly and impersonally spoken, was often to be my first greeting from an islander.

'And tell me now, iss this the first time you are here?'

The curiosity was detached but sincere, inviting further explanation. I said something about filthy weather and late ferries, then asked please where a Mr Macdonald might be found. I was sorry to seem in a hurry but then you see Mr Macdonald was expecting me.

'Well my name itself is Mr Macdonald.' I might have supplied the 'And I'm not expecting you at all', but the old man smiled in gentle amusement. 'We're all Macdonalds, here.' Of course, the Macdonalds of the islands. I gave more details.

'Ah yes, its Murdo Iain Macdonald, Glebe, that you're after. A second cousin of mine. A fine man, O aye, a grand fellow.'

The old man in his own good time gave me clear directions. Five miles to Bayhead, and then The Glebe was on my right at the top of a steep hill. The house stood far back from the road and the turning was through white gateposts.

'Don't worry, he won't be expecting you at any particular time. And chust you tell him I wass asking after him.'

Bayhead was no more than a gathering of the croft-houses which had lined the road all the way up this west side of the island and I

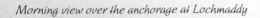
Morning view over the anchorage at Lochmaddy

Cottage at Vallay

wondered just what differentiated a Hebridean township from its apparently densely populated croftland. The presence of a telephone kiosk perhaps, or another unattended petrol pump. Bayhead straggled on northwards and at some indefinite point became Balranald and Hougharry. My headlights picked up the white gateposts at the side of the road and I turned between them up a stony track to The Glebe.

I patted a rough collie which grinned, shook Mrs Macdonald's hand and stepped into a kitchenful of family. There was Mrs Macdonald herself, Mary as I was to know her, sturdy and capable, doing all the introductions. Her husband, Murdo, half rose from a bench by the stove, gave my hand a dry strong clasp and sat down again, smiling. A young woman, their daughter Susan, dandled a baby at the table, and seated behind the table against the wall were two sons, Iain and Donald. I was invited to the table and between the small talk of introduction gathered my first impression of a Hebridean crofting family in its kitchen environment.

Murdo was a small, lean man, probably in his sixties. He spoke little and then in emphatic bursts, the words half hidden by a laugh. Laughter and emphasis were both a result of shyness: he was a man of action rather than easy conversation. What seemed unusual, but later I found universal among crofters at home, was his habit of wearing cap, overalls and boots indoors. Murdo had passed his leanness on to his sons, but they had their mother's tallness and air of capable self-sufficiency. Iain, in his early twenties, was aloof but obviously interested in the stranger. Donald, in his teens, was silent and turned away, excessively shy. He was still at school, travelling each day to the junior secondary in Benbecula. Iain worked the croft with his father and a third son, Kenneth, was in Inverness training to be a policeman. It was a pattern repeated in many crofting families. The eldest son works the croft and inherits it; the younger sons leave the island in order to further their education or find employment on the mainland. Susan was at The Glebe only temporarily, being on holiday from husband and home in Glasgow. She was a typical crofter's daughter, plump, dark, vivacious, happily obsessed with her child. A younger daughter, Morag, was absent, working as a trainee nurse in Dundee.

My immediate impression was of a family tightly knit in spite of its inevitable dispersal. Not prosperous, but respectable and somehow steady, showing the typical Scottish reverence for 'getting on' in life, even though this meant getting away from the island.

This responsible attitude towards life was founded in the mother, Mrs Macdonald. Of the family, she was the exceptional one, the personality which influenced them all and supplied direction. The children took after her in looks, being tall, small headed, dark haired and dark eyed. The facial resemblance was quite distinctive, all·having broad prominent cheekbones and faces rather short between forehead and chin, making eyes seem large and mouths wide. The boys were slim where mother and daughter were rounded, but plump or slim all had long strong bones, their working hands unexpectedly long-fingered and sensitive. Mother and offspring also had in common a physical aloofness; not withdrawal or shyness, but more an extreme reserve, as if they held themselves away in their height and used their dark colouring as a shadow from which to watch and assess. Although aloof, they created an atmosphere of polite enquiry which was stimulating rather than intrusive.

The kitchen surprised me. From outside, the house through the rain had suggested a modern detached bungalow, suburban rather than Highland. Nearly all the croft-houses passed on the way were like this, as if taken from some council housing scheme near a city and scattered each behind its own wire fence and housing estate garden gate, across the rough fields of the island. The only thing distinguishing these island houses from their city counterpart were the black windy distances between them. Stepping over the threshold of The Glebe I half expected an electric fire and a tawdry up-to-dateness of fittings and furniture. But The Glebe kitchen which expressed and mainly housed the Macdonalds was as removed from the cheap suburban as were the people themselves.

Placed against the wall opposite the outside door, but dominating the kitchen and seeming central to it, was a vast ancient peat-burning stove. It was made of heavy iron, all black and shiny with much polishing. Pipes of the same weighty cast iron ran from the stove into the wall behind and the old iron made the new plaster walls seem ridiculously flimsy. The doors of the stove hung open and red heat from the burning peats thrust itself between the thick iron bars of the grate. No flame was visible, only this pulsing red of the peats; no smoke or charred residue, only fine ash, flocculent, grey, light as goosedown, drifting rather than dropping onto a metal tray. To one side of the grate was a large bread oven and the top of the stove held several hot-plates always available for boiling kettles or other cooking. The household water was also heated from the stove, so there was always plenty of hot water in the taps. The peat which provided all this heat stood in a bucket on the floor and it seemed to me that the stove turned the kitchen into a sort of engine room: I imagined Mrs Macdonald shovelling peats, sending heat and energy through all the house.

The kitchen also contained a large double sink, a Calor gas cooker and a plain wooden table with many simple chairs positioned at random. Murdo's bench fitted neatly between stove and wall and when the stove was burning, as tonight, it must have provided the hottest of seats.

Above our heads on the walls were deep shelves supporting all shapes and sizes of tins, tubs, bottles and bins, and plates with other crockery were stacked on a kitchen dresser near the sink. It was not a tidy kitchen, but neither was it squalid: it was a combination of work-room and living-room, a place for family togetherness either in daily work or evening relaxation.

I soon felt at my ease, in Macdonald's kitchen. After an initial few minutes, when I was the centre of attention, the family's natural curiosity relaxed and they talked among themselves. They spoke in Gaelic, apologising to me; it wasn't that they wanted to hide anything, just that they always talked this way. The Gaelic conversation had a fluency which it lost whenever English was used for my benefit. Murdo's speech and indeed his whole manner relaxed when Gaelic was being used, as though this signified a return to normality, the security of family and kitchen. I did not feel excluded

Spinning is still common on North Uist: here the spinners are using wool dyed with crottle, a yellow lichen

when they spoke in Gaelic; on the contrary, this implied an acceptance of my presence, and I was more able to relax. Susan's baby crawled onto my knee and I gathered it up, held it against me and was grateful for its warmth, ingenuous trusting of itself to my stranger's hands. Through the thin hair of the child, I watched the adult members of the family and tried to understand them, if not their language.

When the RSPB acquired Balranald reserve in 1966, a well-known Scottish ornithologist with a special affection for the area donated a caravan for use as warden's accommodation. I had been told in Edinburgh that the caravan was small, antiquated and had not been in prime condition in 1966. By now, it might be decidedly disreputable. The society at that time quite cheerfully acknowledged that wardens' accommodation generally was substandard. Houses for permanent staff on year-round reserves were dubious, but very much better than the various huts, bothies, caravans or other similar forms of accommodation offered to temporary wardens on a seasonal reserve. The society expected the wardens to understand that economy in expenditure on housing was for the greater cause of nature conservation. Surprisingly enough, most wardens sympathised and accepted their poor living conditions without much complaint. As for accommodation for temporary staff on seasonal reserves, the society pointed out that the wardens always expected to move on and therefore took no pride in, or care of what housing was provided. Some wardens were more careful than others. The Balranald caravan had had its good and bad seasons like the rest. It had to stand outdoors all winter and in the stormy, salty Hebrides this was much to its disadvantage; on the other hand, it was looked after in the warden's absence by the Macdonalds, who might effect minor repairs and would certainly report any major damage. No one from HQ had visited the reserve during the last two years so no one knew exactly what condition the caravan was in. Since nothing to the contrary had been reported by the Macdonalds, it was assumed that the caravan was still on site and intact.

After my day's travelling and a couple of hours at The Glebe, I was too tired to remember any misgivings about the possible state of the caravan. Mrs Macdonald had made tea; I had drunk several black sweet cups of it and eaten many substantial home-baked

scones thickly spread with butter, cheese, jam. Then she had produced their special fruit cake. I was full and dozing in my chair
when Iain gently reminded me that The Glebe, after all, was not my
home, so was I perhaps ready to be taken to the caravan?

Iain drove ahead in The Glebe's white pick-up. It was still raining
and blowing hard. We jolted down the main road, crossed it and
went down a narrow uneven track between wire fences for a mile
until we reached a fingerpost pointing left to Goular. An even
narrower track brought us after a quarter of a mile to the caravan, a
blue tin box with wheels, ominously secured to the ground by taut
steel hawsers. We swung our vehicles off the track onto the grass by
the caravan and Iain led the way in. It stank of damp and mould and
when Iain lit the gas mantle I saw that it was tiny, the smallest area in
which I had ever been asked to live since the days of playpen and
cradle. Iain helped me to transfer my belongings from the van and
when this was done the living space was even less. That was a problem for tomorrow; all I needed for the moment was a space to
spread a sleeping bag and to achieve this heaped everything in the

25

kitchen space on the central table. Outside, as we said goodnight, I sensed a great spaciousness around me, a vastness of wind-filled night.

'What's that roaring noise?' I asked.

Iain listened intently. 'Och man' he said, 'That's nothing. That's the sea.' Then he drove away up the track and I was alone.

Gales and rain were to keep me awake often in the caravan and elsewhere on Uist. That first night I slept soundly simply because I was exhausted. And next morning the weather hadn't lifted at all; I woke early to the thunderous noise of wind against metal walls and rain hammering on the roof. There was little to entice me out of bed; obviously I couldn't go outside and the interior of the caravan was in a hideous mess. My belongings lay where heaped the previous evening: suitcases containing clothes and papers, boxes of books and food, a rucksack bulky with miscellaneous domestic and optical equipment. Somewhere in this tiny caravan space must be found for all this stuff and everything would have to be methodically stored, since lack of method and domestic discipline leads to a misery of chaos in a caravan. From my prone position between wall and table I assessed the facilities. Storage space appeared to be confined to a narrow and extremely flimsy plywood shelf above the opposite window and a small kitchen cupboard. The living area was slightly shorter than me when lying down and about half as wide; the kitchen was miniscule, a few feet square, and that little space was mostly taken up by a Calor gas cooker and two large cylinders. There was no working surface in the kitchen and the living area had only this small, presumably folding, table and two built-in seats on one of which I must sleep. The inadequate living and storage area was further reduced; the caravan was leaking badly, rainwater seaped in at each weather corner and a drip from the kitchen ceiling hit the top of one of my suitcases. There were pools of water on the floor.

Somewhere in here clothing must be stored, some of it outdoor stuff and bulky to meet the cold and wet of an island summer. There were several score of books to shelve, which had to be kept dry, and also official papers and stationery. Food would fill the cupboard several times over. I lay there, pondering, while the caravan swayed and creaked and rain streamed down the steamed up windows. How had the previous wardens coped with the lack of space? Or had they all been insouciant hardy young ornithologists used to travelling light? Another problem occurred to me with growing urgency: what about a toilet? Iain hadn't mentioned one and there was nothing inside the caravan. What, indeed, about water; no one had mentioned that either and hopefully it wouldn't always be supplied by the leak in the ceiling.

Resisting the temptation to lie there getting more and more depressed, I struggled out of the sleeping-bag and sat at the table. In order to take my first look at the North Uist landscape I had first to wipe the windows clear of steam, then adjust my eyes to window

panes blurred by rain and shaken in their frames by the wind. A landscape seen from indoors, distorted by wind and rain, the perspective seemed uncomfortably significant.

The rear of the caravan faced east, inland. A track led up to the main road and The Glebe, running straight and slightly uphill. The foreground was flat stubble fields and wire fences, and about a quarter of a mile away to the left were the houses of Hougharry township. Beyond fields and township was a line of low hills, blurred by rain. Occasionally the rounded summits of these hills were scraped by cloud. Village, fields and hills were repellent but not alarming, and slightly to the right of the point where the track went out of sight over the fields was an isolated white croft-house, probably The Glebe. I had human contact, if not yet friends, in that direction.

By turning myself completely around and kneeling against the seat, I could study the view from the caravan southwards. The grassy level on which the caravan stood was bounded by the track and a fence of two strands of barbed wire, five of plain, running across the entire prospect. On the other side of the fence the land dipped gradually to what appeared to be some sort of marsh or agricultural wasteland. It wasn't exactly wetland or pasture, just vegetation longer than normal for a field and some patches of surface water. Around and among the marshy hollows were drier hummocks with rocks. The celebrated Balranald marshes spread south of Goular; that land on the other side of the fence was the climactic centre of the nature reserve, the whole reason for my being here. It looked no more than a stretch of peculiarly misused farmland.

The kitchen window looked westwards and here the track ran on through a gate and across another fenced field of stubble, to a ruined church and cemetery. Stark on the top of a small hill the church was the only dramatic feature in the entire outlook from the caravan. Two tall pointed gable ends were linked by crumbling walls and around the church stood or leaned ancient tombstones. It was like something out of a Gothic horror story, this decaying but still menacing remnant set vertical against sweeps of flat fields and sky. The land beyond the church was the 'machair' I had heard and read about, but had been unable to visualise. Through the rainy caravan window it was just an area of uncompromisingly flat fields, like a lot of football pitches placed side by side minus the goalposts, ending a mile or so away in a long ragged-topped ridge of even height. Peering intently at the raggedness of this ridge I noticed that it quivered and realised that the vegetation was marram grass and the ridge an unbroken bank of sand-dunes.

The remaining window looked north and was filled with what was left of the township called Goular. A few yards from the caravan stood a croft-house and byre. Very small, walls rounded against wind, tiny windowed and roofed with lichenous decaying slates, it looked more like a mossy rock than a house. Attached to the stone building was a shed of flapping and rusting corrugated tin. To one side and slightly behind these was a ruined house or byre, walls falling down and roof timbers askew against the sky. Another empty but less ruinous cottage stood by a track which led from the township across the machair, and set back from this track and the rest of the township was Goular's only permanently occupied dwelling, a substantial two-storied house built of granite, then nothing but black rainy sky. Though I couldn't see it, a hundred yards from the caravan was the horseshoe curve of Hougharry Bay, then open sea.

Nothing attracted me outside, especially at that early hour and in such foul weather. There seemed every reason to grope back into the sleeping-bag like some animal into a warm strawy nest, there to doze away the morning – or the day, or however long it might take for the weather to lift. But a couple of pints of Mrs Macdonald's strong tea begged for release. I swore to myself, pulled on wellingtons and waterproof and went exploring.

Over flat fields the houses of Hougharry watched me with windows like unblinking eyes. Obviously they disapproved. I searched around and eventually found concealment in the ruined byre. Wind came chilly through gaps in old walls, the roof timbers looked ready to collapse. Clambering around inside over heaps of mortar, slates, wallstones and broken glass, I thought how absurd if wardens since 1966 had had to do this every morning. Or were they unusually trained in retention? I would enquire delicately of Iain. A dozen black bullocks were grouped possessively around a metal tap and a wooden tub at the trackside, my water supply. I slopped through cattle muck and mud to the tap and turned it. The water was clear. It was difficult to catch any because of the wind, but at last I cupped some in my hands and tasted. It was excellent water, with a taste of salt in the cold sweetness.

By mid-morning I had organised the interior of the caravan. It was still congested and there would be problems in the weeks ahead when I would be spending most of my time outdoors, coming in wet and too tired to give domestic jobs proper attention. But I found an unsuspected underseat cavity for my clothes and improvised more bookshelf space using my empty cardboard boxes. Tins of food just had to stand on the floor. Some official documents remained in my suitcase which was wedged under the table. That tiny living space was sitting-room, study, office and bedroom all in one; some time in the near future it would have to receive birdwatching visitors to the reserve, but that problem could be put out of mind for the present.

It had all taken considerable effort and ingenuity. I eased my knees sideways and placed my elbows on the table between type-writer and breadbin, and wondered what to do next.

At the RSPB's Scottish headquarters in Edinburgh, I had been briefed by the director and his assistant regarding my main duties during the forthcoming season. As a matter of routine common to every reserve, I must make regular bird counts and census the breeding bird population. There was protection of rare species to be organised and the instruction and supervision of birdwatching visitors. Good relations with crofters and other landowners must be maintained.

In addition to these conventional duties, it had fallen to me to improve the warden's accommodation and visitor reception facilities at Balranald. Previous wardens had lived in the caravan and received visitors at the door; but this system was inadequate and the society had recently acquired the small croft-house which stood nearby. The house was rented from an absentee; the shed was the property of the sole remaining member of Goular township, an old man called Cameron who had once owned the cottage, but now lived in the larger house on the shore.

The shed was to be demolished, the two-roomed cottage converted, one room to house a warden, the other for storage and visitor reception. Since most materials and tools for such building work would be unavailable on the island, I must assess the minimum required and it would be sent with furniture from Edinburgh. The assistant director himself would attend to the purchase of my requirements and bring everything to Uist later in the season.

It was suggested that the early part of the season should be devoted to the bird censusing and first assessment of the newly acquired buildings. By midsummer the bird activity would be past its climax but this would be my busiest time with visitors. When the holiday season ended in late August I could begin repairs on the cottage.

My season was roughly planned. But there was much for me to learn about the warden's role at Balranald and many of its birds were unfamiliar. To inform me further I was supplied with a thick wad of typed foolscap, the complete file of previous wardens' monthly and annual reports. A rainy day such a this was a fortunate opportunity to read these reports.

Starting with the 1966 season, I began to read and read all day entirely absorbed. By evening I was eyesore but better informed. There was much to learn and most of my knowledge of both birds and wardenship would only be acquired by experience as the season passed.

Curlew

Wind shook the caravan and rain beat down on it all that night. It was hardly credible that the weather could worsen, but it did. At dawn next morning the rain was just as heavy and the wind stronger, like some great fist shaking and pummelling, punishing me personally for coming here. I woke early but lay in bed for a long time, staring at a patch of dark grey formless sky through the skylight. The impulse was to burrow deep down, sleep again and wake up elsewhere; perhaps in Wales, at Ynys-hir, to a view of oak trees and estuary; or better still, at home in Inverness, to the sound of the kettle boiling downstairs, greenfinches chirping in the garden and morning sunshine slanting across the lawn.

During the night, wind had rocked the caravan so much that the cupboard door had sprung open and the contents cascaded to the floor. I'd heard the crash but had ignored it because there was no point in groping around in the dark. Now there were broken eggs mixed with jam and coffee, and tins rolling around in the mess. Fortunately there was no broken glass, so I scooped it all up, washed the floor and replaced the tins. Breakfast was coffee-flavoured scrambled eggs sweetened with strawberry jam – the all-in-one morning meal.

Grimly eating, I faced the west window of the caravan and saw a lot of grey sky and Cameron's unattractive croft-house. I must see Cameron to ask his Christian name for documents relating to the sale of his decrepit barn to the RSPB. He also kept the key to the building to be renovated.

I had seen nothing of Cameron since my arrival and there was no sign of him now. No smoke from his chimney, no light from his windows, although it must be dark in there on such a morning. The house was daunting and so was the gale-filled, rain-beaten hundred yards between it and the caravan. In their reports, previous wardens had unanimously stressed the importance of getting on well with the crofters. To establish friendly relations I would have to overcome natural reticence and go out and meet them, even knock on a few closed croft-house doors. To meet Cameron was a first and obvious necessity.

Opening the caravan door required both hands to stop the wind whipping it off its hinges and a shoulder to shove the door shut. Turning the corner of the byre into the wind was like walking into a wall of wet glass. This was my first experience of a Hebridean gale, one of those winds which march furiously across the North Atlantic and treat the islands like episodes of mid-ocean. It tasted of salt and was icily cold. Like some boxer against a superior opponent, I staggered, weaved, dodged, ducked, side-stepped and doubled up against a barrage of blows. I considered giving up, retreating to my caravan corner and throwing in some metaphorical sponge. Then my hands met wire, I grabbed with the other and was hanging to Cameron's fence, flapping there like washing. Cameron obviously wouldn't take me in to dry so I battled hand over hand along his fence to the gate. There was no question of opening this string and wire structure, I just bundled anyhow over it and, with a crouching run, reached the house. There, in the comparative shelter of the doorway, I wiped salty rain and wind tears from my face, straightened my dishevelled waterproofs and tried to compose myself. I rapped on the wooden door with bare knuckles. The sound was lost in a howl of wind, one with rain on the roof and rattling slates. Hanging for support on the metal door-ring with one hand, I hammered with all my strength on the door with the other. Much more of this and I'll break wrists or smash knuckles. Inside the house a dog barked. It sounded a long way off, as if shut up behind many closed doors. The barking stopped.

Once more, and summoning strength, I hammered again, laid my head against the wood and listened. The dog renewed its barking but there was no other response. A noise which might just have been a door being scraped open somewhere inside, held me. Silence again, the silence of wind. At last a sort of sliding, shuffling noise as if something heavy was being dragged through the house.

The noise approached the outer door and I stepped back instinctively. Whatever it was inside seemed to reach the door and proceed to claw its way upwards towards the ring. I didn't know what to expect, whether to wait there or turn and run; but I stayed, fascinated by the noise and the slow turning of the ring. The door opened an inch. I flung myself towards the opening and began yelling.

'Hello, hello, Mr Cameron.'

The gap opened wider and, windy though it was, I could smell the interior of the house: a strongly lavatorial air with traces of decaying foodstuff, stale sweat and paraffin. Framed against the doorway and his stinks stood Cameron, a monument to decrepitude and self-neglect. He was short and seemed shorter because so bowed, and clung to the doorway as if for support. His face was sunken, a strange yellow in colour, darkened by dirt and unshaven beard, deeply lined and unspeakably senile. His mouth hung open, his loose lips dribbled frothy spit. He wore a grey cheap suit, trousers and jacket both caked with grease and sweat, and down the trouser front was a wide stain of urine. Under the suit was a filthy, shapeless jersey which, like the suit, hung on him as if made for someone treble his height and girth. A cloth cap was wedged down on his head, thrusting forward already prominent, bushy eyebrows, and on his feet were slippers which explained the slithering sound of his approach. Had he lifted his feet, the slippers would have fallen to pieces.

Cameron didn't seem one bit pleased to see me. In fact he looked just like some savage house dog, antagonistic but too ruinously old to bite. He said nothing, only frowned as I recovered enough to gabble out my name, that I was the new warden in the caravan. The brow wrinkled and the eyebrows projected even further. Still he

Winter view of Lochmaddy Bay

said nothing. His hand, which hung from the side of the door, was emaciated, dirt encrusted, and with black fingernails grown into hooks. It was like the claw of some long-dead predatory bird. Staring hard at the hand I asked Cameron if he would tell me his name, please, his Christian name. I stopped babbling and the silence became intense. Cameron gathered himself to some extreme pitch of resentment and finally spat out a single word, 'Airrchibald!', then he slammed the door in my face.

I bundled back to the caravan a great deal faster than I had come, retrieved my seat by the window and felt exceedingly miserable. There was nothing to relieve my mood from any of the windows; rain was sheeting down over the marshes, machair and township, and there was no sign in the sky of any clearance. Someone in the south once told me that all young enterprising crofters emigrated, leaving only the incompetent and the aged, a sort of natural selection causing degeneracy. The township of Hougharry again seemed deserted. Was it populated mainly by people like Cameron, in every one of those houses some elderly misanthrope squalidly dying? If so, what earthly chance was there of making a success of the 'public relations' aspect of my job?

I had forgotten, of course, about The Glebe Macdonalds. Cameron could never be a true representative of island type if people so obviously vital and likable lived here. As if to remind me of this, Iain appeared at that lowest of my moments on his way to feed Glebe cattle on the machair. He was seated on a tractor without a cab and drawing a trailer and he wore a yellow seaman's sou'wester suit against the weather. I waved at him through the window and he stopped the tractor beside the caravan, gesturing towards the trailer behind in an invitation to jump in. I landed on a heap of rain-soaked oat-sheaves.

The weather was too bad for me to note where we were going, but Iain drove through two gates and across some trackless uneven surface for a few minutes, to reach his cattle. The beasts were already gathered round, the more insistent animals leaning into the trailer, plucking at the sheaves. Seeing me among the oats, they rolled their eyes with fright and jerked away. Iain bawled instructions to me and I clambered to my feet, holding the trailer tailboard with one hand and throwing sheaves with the other. We moved on until there was a curved trail of oat-sheaves about a hundred yards long across the field. The cattle lumbered from sheaf to sheaf, snatching at them with long anxious lips, sometimes throwing them up in an eagerness of acute hunger. Chaff scattered downwind, across flat stubble which ended in a line of sand-dunes.

After even such brief exposure to the wind my hands were rawly red and numbed; they also stung from handling the rough sheaves. As the cattle settled to feed, the raindrops, made into missiles by the wind, struck and glistened on already saturated pelts. They were small animals, long haired but not so shaggy or wide-horned as postcard Highland cattle. They looked bony and in generally poor condition, but how hardy they must be to survive at all. They had no shelter, only the flat field in which to stand or lie, close together to break the wind and spread a little warmth, all the long day and longer nights; those mainland cattle were cosseted by comparison.

We bumped back to the caravan. Iain came in and occupied my seat. Handing a mug of tea to Iain, I noticed how large was his hand and how he grasped the mug without discomfort although it was scaldingly hot. Work hardens and develops any hand, and wind and rain must swell joints to make the islanders' hands preternaturally large. In his bulky waterproofs, Iain seemed to fill the caravan.

'And how are you liking this weather?' he asked.

I told him not at all and also about my morning meeting with Cameron. Iain shook his head disapprovingly.

'You should never have tried it today. He's hardly likely to be at his best in this weather, the poor creature. Try him when the sun's out; you'll find he's not so bad as you think.'

This seemed wise. That early visit was presumptuous, altogether foolish. Iain's words eased my mind about Cameron, but on the subject of another sort of easement he was less helpful.

'Toilet? Ach, man, there's plenty toilets, down the machair.'

Too long spent sedentary indoors, the blood stagnates and the mind has a tendency to brood darkly, inwards. A walk would do me good even if it was a rain-beaten crawl.

I plunged out of the caravan into water and wind and took the track leading past the caravan and Cameron's house to the machair. Direction didn't really matter since I couldn't see anything anyway.

The track was hard sand, worn into parallel ruts by vehicles, with a strip of grass between. On my left were the flat fields of stubble and the sand-dunes ranged by Iain's cattle; no doubt they had finished their oat-sheaves by now and were hungering. Lowering my head against the wind I plodded on: at my feet, the whitest sand I had ever seen and here on the track it was compressed hard as cement. To my right the land rose through rough pasture grasses to a near skyline of wind-tortured marram and beyond it was a drop to Hougharry Bay. Sounds of wind and sea were inseparable in all that stormy roaring, but I sensed the Atlantic out there, felt its tumult, and on my lips was the taste of salt.

After a while the land broadened out and became fields or, rather, less fields than stubble plains criss-crossed by wire fencing; a small version of mid-America, a Hebridean oat prairie. Dunes in the west seemed no nearer and, goodness, what a featureless landscape it was; and what an impoverished prairie, the soil between the winter-bitten rows of stubble was almost pure sand, no dark earth at all and virtually no grass. Some patches were evidently fallow and they were even sandier than the stubble; a mere tracery of the wiriest and spikiest grass survived there, all that remained no doubt after a whole winter of grazing by rabbits, sheep and cattle.

Plumes of sand above the marram snaked high, then were wind caught and flung downwards towards the fields. Hundreds of yards from the dunes sand grains pattered my oilskins, were sharper on face and hands than rain, white sand writhing under a dead grey sky, over a featureless stubble plain. I had seen photographs of snows eternally streaming from Himalayan summits and sand-storms in hot deserts; they were the extreme wildernesses of our world but they seemed no more desolate than this machair.

At first the sea took all my attention. Three days of storms had built waves up to massive proportions and now they plunged land-wards with fearful towering regularity. Not a choppy sea, with its power dispersed into distinct white-topped wavelets, cut about by crosswinds and currents, but one huge curve of inimical blue-green following another, slowly and rhythmically mounting and curling and pouring down, streaming from the apex of each curl. It was serene in its huge strength, that sea. It seemed almost caressive, not destructive at all. Or rather it was neither, having no reference to

The view from Balranald overlooking Bayhead: on the horizon are Mount Eaval (left) and South Uist (right)

humankind, existing only for itself with no ulterior purpose. I saw how beautiful it was and was utterly appalled.

At shore level, the sea towered above me higher than ever. The sound of individual waves breaking was lost in the tone of the whole sea, a deep thunderous roar without source or direction. But by then the sky was beginning to break from its all-over grey into clouds and blue spaces and it was as impressive as the sea. It was the sort of sky I came later to call 'cumulus and blue' and I have never been more aware of these skies than over the Outer Hebrides. Not only do they occur more often there, created by processional cyclones across the North Atlantic, but you quite simply see more of them because the skies are incomparably tall and wide. West is sea all the way to America and North Uist in particular is mainly flat, so that standing anywhere on the island you have almost 180 degrees of sky arching from horizon to horizon, from the blue-black ruler straight line of the sea, up and overhead and down to the hills which are distanced to a mere peripheral serration.

In minutes, weather and scene had undergone one of those transformations for which the islands are famed: from grey opacity to blue and white, crystalline. Looking west were islands read about

but never seen: of the Monachs I could see only half of the light-house, the islands being machair flat and the sea that morning mountainous; but St Kilda's summit overtops its 1,000ft seacliffs by 600ft and, though 40 sea miles away, it was splendidly clear.

I rested awhile on the sand and then moved north, following a low, rocky coastline. This was the beginning of Ard an Runair, a headland which juts from the machairs of Hougharry and Balranald. It is a protective rocky tip to a hinterland of sandy machair and is the westernmost extremity of mainland North Uist – the edge not only of Uist, but of Britain and indeed the European continent. Yesterday's reading of wardens' reports made me feel already quite familiar with the headland which, because of its wes-terly position, is an attractive resting place for migrant birds. All previous wardens had reported sightings of rarities from here, storm-blown vagrants from both America and Europe, probably exhausted, near death, but finding some temporary rest among the headlands, outcrops and inlets. Signs of an important skua migra-tion had been detected up the coast past Ard an Runair and geese of several species were known to congregate in large flocks, using the headland as a stop-off spot on route for Iceland and Greenland,

Exploring Balranald

their breeding grounds in the Arctic. That first day on Ard an Runair I was cold, wind-buffeted, and wouldn't have spotted a rare migrant at my feet. Later I was to walk there over sweet sun-warmed turf and daisies so thickly in flower that from a distance they looked like snowfields; and I came to believe that Ard an Runair was prominent in wardens' reports not because it was good for birds, but because of all the reserve it was the place where wardens chose to spend their time.

Between the tip of the headland and Eilean Trostain, island of otters, was a channel crossable on foot only at times of low spring tides, 40yd of seaweed-draped boulders where a big crab might lurk, even a lobster. A fine hunting ground for otters then, but today I couldn't imagine anything living in either the channel or out on the wind-scoured island. Nothing living – then I rubbed wind tears from my eyes and refocused on a yellowish cluster of foam among the rocks. It moved, it shook itself without disintegrating downwind. Not foam but a sheep, and there were more along the shore of the island, a few lying in grassy hollows above. Days later Iain told me that they were not stranded but deliberately ferried there by crofters in Hougharry. Grass, incredibly, often sprouts green on such islands earlier in spring than on adjacent coasts and

Hooded crows

Otter

the sheep are grazed there for this early bite. If the grass is in short supply, the sheep will follow ebbing tides as far as they can for the succulent mid-channel seaweeds. A lot of iron, iodine and other nutrient in the deeper sea wracks helps ewes through a wintry lambing. Not knowing all this, to me the tiny island looked uninviting, even by a sheep's standards.

Trostain is part of the Balranald bird reserve, as is the island of Causamul, 3 miles further west. Causamul is larger than Trostain but even less hospitable. Swept by high seas most of the winter, it is a true outlier and has a characteristic fauna and flora. Seals breed there as do puffins and, it was rumoured, that most pelagic of birds, the storm petrel. Waves pounded on Causamul's rocks and spray leapt twice the height of its summit cairn. Causamul would have to be inspected one day. Under present conditions, Ard an Runair was adventure enough.

The wind hustled me back along the north coast of the headland and threw sand at me across the head of Hougharry Bay, but it was a rainless wind now and blustery rather than constant. The storm was blowing itself out. I clambered up the steep loose face of sand from beach to machair and only a hundred yards away sat my own township, Goular: Cameron's grim house, a ruckle of ruins and my caravan, all insignificant compared to the derelict church and cemetery nearby. A place more for the dead than the living.

Although Cameron was non-evident as before, there was some stir of life about the old buildings. Sheep clattered out of the ruined house, in their fright bringing down more roof spars and stones from the walls. A pair of crows were playing in wind gusts over the church. Not the familiar black carrion crows of southern Britain or lowland Scotland, but the grey crows or 'hoodies' of the Highlands and islands. In spring and especially in late afternoon or evening sunlight, the grey of their plumage can appear pinkish. They can be rosy birds, the crows; but it is the devil's fire that is in them, for they are even more rapacious than the black crows of the South.

The crows were joined by a pair of fulmar petrels and the four birds began a battle over the church gables that was half play, half serious dispute over territory. The fulmars were prospecting for a nest site which they might not fully occupy until May, but the crows had already started gathering sticks and lengths of dried sea-weed from the shore to a flat-topped corner of the walls. The crows flapped and squawked; the fulmars were graceful, weaving silently.

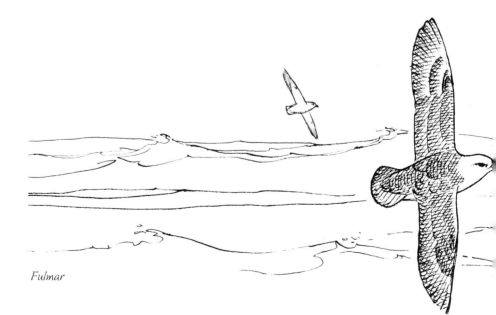

Fulmar

They look passive birds, fulmars, less angular and milder eyed than the large seagulls they otherwise resemble. They sweep round impersonally on stiffly out-held short wings and they are almost voiceless except to each other at the nest site. Yet as a species they are successful and expanding colonists, and as individuals they can by sheer silent persistence oust much larger birds. Peregrine falcons have been known to give way to them, as have greater black-backs, biggest and most powerful of the gulls. If the fulmars were determined to nest on the church, the rowdy bellicosity of the crows wouldn't stop them.

In the caravan, I made a very large pot of tea and drank all of it before getting round to an evening meal. The meal was more substantial than usual. Appetite for both food and drink was to be greatly increased by island life. Strong winds, sharp salty air and a demanding environment explained the crofters' notorious preference for stodgy, starchy foods, scones and potatoes, and with much strong drink, black tea or whisky.

Sipping tea and later, while eating, I saw more inhabitants of Goular. Beyond the fence a patch of floodwater had been deepening and widening since morning. This was an arm of the famous Balranald marshes, a part of which would dry out later in the season and become an area of iris beds and rush clumps. Now it was a small shallow lake with many islands and across it in the evening sunlight came a pair of whooper swans, wild swans which breed in the Arctic but winter numerously in the islands. They came sailing directly across the pool to its edge, then lost their aquatic grace as they climbed out and waddled across the narrow strip of grass between pool and fence. They stopped and pushing their heads through the wires, plucked at the seed heads of the long grass at the track-side, rather like a pair of long-necked, feathered sheep, but wilder than sheep, more musical. As they pulled at the grass they talked; a muted version of the better known bugling calls of skeins in flight. This quieter voice of paired swans together was conversational, endearing. Before dark I also saw my first corn bunting on the island. Small, dumpy, heavy billed, it flew from nowhere among the buildings to perch on the fence near the swans and give a burst of spring song, a dry, monotonous, sandy little song which was to weary me as the season went on. That evening the corn bunting's song was welcome, warming as sunshine. With the soft talk of the swans it helped me to feel less alone.

Whooper swans

In the morning no wind at all and a sky of flawless blue: 1 April, my day as an April fool. Such a morning couldn't be wasted and after breakfast I spread the map of the reserve in sunlight coming warmly through the caravan window to the table. The boundary of the reserve should be walked, my new territory assessed. This is easy enough on three sides where the boundary is the sea-shore with nothing to hinder free walking, but the east and central area of the reserve is more complex and difficult to approach. The inland boundary is a road, but it lies too far from the marshland to give good views of it. It was essential for me to learn how to gain access to the marsh as this would be to any naturalist the most interesting part of the reserve. I stared hard at the map, trying to find some single feature which might allow me to understand better the topography of the whole.

The hub of the marshes seemed to be a 2-mile long stretch of open water called Loch nam Feithean. It all looked fascinatingly confusing on the map, an area of hummocks and hollows, bogs, reedbeds, pools and lagoons. I would have to walk there and find out by trial and error which parts of it would support me, which threaten to drown. The best approach was by western beaches to the estuary of Loch Paible, then up its crooked length to the marsh. At least I would have a dry walk on the sands before engaging with the difficult wetlands.

It was still very early in the morning when I set out from the caravan, maps rolled under arm and binoculars around my neck, swinging. It has been written of island crofters that they sleep reprehensibly late. Certainly there was no one about as I passed Cameron's house and followed a track towards the sea. This was the machair crossed yesterday, considered lifeless. This morning I looked clear across it to croftlands, and beyond green fields studded with houses rose blue island hills: the sharp rocky edge of Eaval in North Uist, the more gradual lift of South Uist's long ridge of mountain culminating in 2,000ft high Ben Mhor. A deeper blue than sky must be the island of Barra, at the other end of the outer island chain. Mountains like a row of needles in the east could be none but the Cuillin of Skye. With a background of mountains to balance its flatness, the machair was scenically transformed. Nor was it lifeless. Corn buntings, sparrows and starlings, and that little island finch, the twite, were in flocks round places where oats had been thrown to cattle. Among trampled straw and splashes of dung the birds clustered like flies, lifting light and cohesive as smoke and settling to scold me from fence posts and wires.

In the absence of trees these fences are the main perches for passerine birds on the machair; many posts had corn buntings advertising breeding territory that morning, and they sang most picturesquely from the handle of a long abandoned plough. I looked at the twites carefully, not being familiar with this bird which is so abundant on the island croftlands. They are as numerous as sparrows and similar to sparrows in shape and colour except for a more upright deportment when perched, a generally darker plumage and a pink tinge at the base of the tail. They called with a twang somehow appropriate to oat straws and fence wires.

Skylark

Further out on the machair, the most evident birds were the skylarks. Over every tussock and old furrow they seemed to be singing, some soaring almost out of sight against cloudless blue, others fluttering only inches from the stubble. All were singing, even those perching on the ground; the whole machair from sea to inland croftland rang and seethed with skylarks and their song. Few people can avoid a feeling of uplift when they hear a skylark sing on a fine morning. I walked the last mile across the machair in a dazed state near to rapture.

Iris beds choke the drainage ditches

The first beach is named in Gaelic Traigh Iar – the long beach. There are many Traigh Iars on the sandy west-facing coasts of the Uists. This was to become my favourite of the Uist strands, walked for the purpose of bird counts and again and again for pleasure. About 1¹/₂ miles long, the beach swept in a gentle crescent from Ard an Runair to another headland, called Hestan, to the south. Hestan is a narrow promontory of sand-dunes becoming rocks at its seaward extremity and that morning it pointed like a long big-knuckled forefinger from Uist towards the Monach Islands.

The upper shore of Traigh Iar is wind-driven shell sand, silkily loose in texture when dry, lifting to a steep wall of sand-dune. The dunes are 20–30ft high in places, separated by sand canyons and all have a crest of marram which blows back in the wind like strong green hair from a white forehead.

Uninterrupted white sand can be pleasing to look at, but it is painfully boring to walk. Tides slip up and down and it accepts the calm day lickings of the sea, in stormy weather its savage pounding. But very little invertebrate life can live there and to any naturalist it looks and feels sterile. At Traigh Iar, however, the lower shore is broken by rocks, skerries which run in sharp-topped ridges at right angles to the sea and divide the sandy strand into a series of coves and bays.

These tiny inlets are delightful: they hold sea pools among the rocks where sea-wracks grow and which have deep ledges like shelves where mussels stack themselves with barnacles, limpets and winkles. The sands between the rocks often hold shallow lagoons of sea-water between tides; in calm weather the sea can curl in and out of these sand pools and leave pellucid mirrors for cloud and sky. Shrimps frisk about in them and sand-patterned flounders merge with the bottom, and they give many wading birds sheltered places to roost or feed.

These splinters of rock on Traigh Iar were fingers of land clutching whatever they could from the sea. From the Atlantic they plucked not only birds and fish but the deep seaweeds which are

(pp50–1) Under threat of rain, crofters work with ancient machines to gather a meagre harvest; (inset) On still summer evenings a corncrake's call can be heard for miles

(left) Eider eggs nestle in down among rocks and thrift

Traigh Jar, the beach at Balranald

torn up in gales and collect in such sheltered places along the shore. Traigh Iar holds millions of tons of this deep sea kelp, which can build into platforms several feet deep and hundreds of yards long. The seaweed rots away and of course it stinks to the heavens, but it can provide food for countless insects, birds and machair cattle. Mineral rich as it is, the Uist crofters used to rely on it as manure for their land.

Because of its westerly position and the fact that it is the north-ernmost of a 50-mile long series of beaches fringing all the Uists and Benbecula, Traigh Iar is an unparalleled collecting ground for birds on migration, especially waders. In spring, countless thousands of birds use this western edge of Europe as a long sandy corridor lead-ing them towards their breeding places in the north. Geese and ducks, and seabirds like auks, skuas and petrels fly by, a little distance out to sea and yet aware of the guiding land. It is there for even strong-winged oceanic birds as refuge from storm or a place to find food. Songbirds, the little whistling, chattering passerines, follow the machair in the absence of suitable scrub, sometimes flocking up in the sand-dune hollows or even behind tussocks of marram. Waders fly by in flocks, but for them these western beaches are a natural feeding ground. Many are coming from similar estuarine habitat in the south, where they have been more or less

Oystercatcher

sedentary all winter. Seas are shallow west of the Outer Hebrides and the beaches have an extensive littoral.

To a wader, Traigh Iar is a little estuary and a highly attractive one, offering a banquet among sea kelp delicacies, sand worms in softer parts of the strand, molluscs and small fish in the rock pools. All types of wader are provided for, from the long-billed curlews and godwits which probe for worms, to the tiny beaked ringed plover and sanderlings which patter about on the hard sands behind ebbing waves, picking miniscules of food from the foam. Oyster-catchers smash open mussels and cockles with their red crow-bar bills, dunlins pick at the tiny snails among the worm casts of the muddier inlets, turnstones delve among shingles and fronds of weeds, and purple sandpipers creep about crab-like among the wracks of headlands and skerries. Sometimes even golden plovers and lapwings, though mainly inland feeders, will be attracted by the frost-free shore and bring their plaintive calls from fields and hills.

Not only does the topography of Traigh Iar provide excellent habitat for wading birds, but it gives a birdwatcher unique opportunity to study them at close quarters. Usually, waders are far out on the open mud-flats or salt-marshes where there is no cover to approach them by and stalking is impossible. Only at extreme high tides do the flocks gather together to roost in places where they might be watched. Birdwatchers use sea walls or farm lanes which by-pass coastal marshes, or cars parked at vantage points wherever a road runs along the shore. Even then, the views of birds are often untypical and unsatisfactory. No wader can be appreciated fully when it is one of a roosting flock of thousands of birds of many species. So many birds give an impression of confusion and distress; they are pressurised by the unusual conditions of the tide and either they are a restless amorphous mass or they are all boringly fast asleep with their heads tucked into their scapulars.

Most of my experience of waders until then was as unidentifiable stipples on distant mud-flats, not much more interesting than worm casts, or in flocks rising and falling miles away at the sea's edge. They might have been smoke, or swarms of insects – an essential component of estuarine atmosphere, but always scenery rather than birds. Yet here, in a little bay contained by fingers of rock, only yards away, was as attractive a gathering of waders as any birdwatcher could wish for. Twenty or thirty sanderlings sprinted up and down the sea's edge, ringed plovers and turnstones foraged in some half-buried kelp, a party of redshanks was bickering, chasing, flying round a sand pool. Curlews stood about on the rocks and a heron which saw me coming lifted and flew lethargically out over the sea.

Further down the beach, over another skerry, was a similar group of waders; a slightly different composition of species, no sanderlings but a godwit with the curlews and some oystercatchers standing apparently asleep knee-deep in a pool. Similar birds but different individuals, different positions and activities, a different background of rocks, sea, sky and outlying islands. There were dozens of such skerries and bays and I could have pottered in and out of them all day, studying the waders. Many hours were happily and usefully spent doing precisely this during my season, but it wasn't simply the birds which addicted me to Traigh Iar. Rather, it was observing the birds so naturally in their setting – the seaweed-draped skerries with the sea curling between, white sands and the curl and fall of waves, the always varying colour and condition of sea and sky and the sometimes visible, often rain-hidden shapes of the islands. The sounds of waders, seagulls, sometimes the moaning of seals, and the sea which could come and go like deep breathing. It was undisturbed by humankind, this world of sands, one of Britain's few wholly natural settings, and it may have been its uniqueness which appealed to me immediately and drew me again and again during my wardening season.

Sanderling

At the southern end of Traigh Iar I climbed into the dunes, sat in a grassy hollow and opened a flask of coffee. Facing inland, and in contrast to natural views of beach and ocean, I now had a prospect over that man-made landscape, the machair. I had read a great deal about machair and its formation, and from my dune top found much of the scene satisfyingly intelligible. It is a simple story, a narrative that links wind and rain, beach, sand-dune, machair and croftland.

The sands which make such splendid beaches along the Atlantic shore of the outer islands are not triturated rock as are most sands around the British coats; the sand here is made partly from the shells of marine animals. Because the sea over the islands is so shallow and stormy, the shells are pounded and ground to the texture of sand, which is piled up by wave action to form beaches along the island's western coast. Gales off the Atlantic then pile the sand up into dunes and carry it far inland.

The basic rock of the islands like North Uist is ancient imperme-able lewissean gneiss, an exceptionally aged granite, and vegetation on such a surface does not rot to a fertile soil but forms acidic peat. The central moorlands of the Uists are like this: uncultivable, un-drainable peat bogs. On the western coast, however, the acidity is meliorated by the influence of the wind-blown alkaline shell sand, and a belt of flat land, light and alkaline enough to be cultivable, is formed contiguous with the coast.

This is machair, that seemingly anomalous strip of plentitude on the very edge of wilderness. It achieves its maximum width and uniformity on the machairs of South Uist, and between the islands the sea has broken in to form extensive inlets or areas which are bare sand when uncovered by the tides.

Between the tidal inlet of Loch Paible in the south and Hougharry Bay in the north, the machair of Balranald and Hougharry is intact and typical. I looked across the centre of this machair from my viewpoint in the dunes and read the machair's topography like the text of a geological and botanical guide.

First, the sand piles up into dunes, loose sanded, sparsely vege-tated. Then the dunes are held by marram grasses, which grow more densely inland until the dunes are stable enough to allow the growth of grass, the fine turf of the machair sward. A broad plain of this sward is now ploughed by crofters for grain crops, mainly oats and rye, and used as common grazing for cattle and sheep in winter.

The machair plain comes to its inland limit in shallow freshwater lochs and marshes; in South Uist, a chain of these marshes shows clearly where water from mountains has been dammed against a sandy machair. In North Uist, the main remnant of this habitat is Loch nam Feithean and its marshes.

The fertility of the land diminishes as the sandy influence lessens. Here, on more stable and rocky ground are the townships and crofts, taking advantage of firmer foundation for buildings and for growing potatoes and hay on the land which is at least sweeter than moorland. The built up area of North Uist, which rather oppressed me on first arrival, is a strip of housing confined between western machairs and moorland. Compared to the uninhabited regions on either side, it occupies a negligible amount of the island.

Wind and sand: they have combined to give man a place on this most exposed of Europe's coastlines. I gained a great satisfaction from perceiving the link between geology, topography, human land use and landscape. It was a story into which it was my job to fit wildlife; to record particularly birds and study their various adaptations to the elements and man.

Mankind was beginning to be evident today on the machair. There was a flash as sunlight caught something metallic near the houses of Hougharry and through binoculars I saw that it was a tractor leaving the township. Two more tractors left the houses and

drove through on to the machair. They each had a small plough attached and they came slowly over the stubble to the first tractor with its trailer full of bags. The vehicles parked together and there was a companionable mixing of people. Another tractor left the township, and a fourth, each carrying a plough. One man carried bags to the ends of last year's furrows where the stubble showed clearly discernible strips. Each strip was about a dozen yards wide and ran from the ridge where the vehicles were parked to a fence at the edge of the marsh. A bag was placed at the end of each strip. Four tractors were now grouped on the ridge and the people were setting the ploughs ready for work. Another tractor with plough was coming along the track and a sixth was just leaving the township.

It was the beginning of spring ploughing and sowing. Strips belonged to each crofting family and were ploughed three years, left one year fallow. Each family would have several strips, their location on the machair decided by historic agreement, and scattered so that each family had its share of good and bad land. In a book I read recently about the islands, in which the author had been deprecatory about the primitive island agriculture, it was stated that even

the contemporary crofter has no affinity with machinery. He described how at the beginning of each season the crofter simply backs up to the spot where he abandoned the plough at the end of the ploughing season – it might be in a shed, but more often the plough is left outside somewhere, near the house or on the machair, often simply at the end of the last furrow to be ploughed. The plough is ungreased, rusty, its wheels and discs may be jammed by old straw, the blade may be inches in the ground. But the crofter simply hitches plough to tractor, hauls it out of its winter position and expects it to work immediately, after less attention than would be given to a spade. Crofters understand spades, opined the author, but not ploughs and certainly not tractors. I stretched lazily in the warm April sunshine. This morning I sympathised with non-mechanical proclivities.

After Traigh Iar, the next section of the west boundary was another beach, 1½ miles of dazzling sand called on the map Port na Scalpaig. I came to know it simply as Balranald beach since it is most easily reached by a track which runs past Balranald township and House. It is the most perfectly symmetrical of all the Uist beaches, two crescents of sand meeting like the mid point of a W in a skerry. At high tide the bay can be blue sea up to the base of an unbroken rim of dunes; at low tide it is a silver sickle laid at the land's edge, blade turned towards the sea. Lovely as it is, and though during hot census walks an excellent place to bathe, Balranald beach never attracted me as did Traigh Iar. The sands were too clean, there wasn't enough skerry to give variety, to collect seaweeds, smells and birds.

At the end of the beach a grassy headland curved gradually inland. This was the mouth of Loch Paible, the tidal inlet which is the southern boundary of the reserve. Here the sands change character, become softer and peat stained, more like estuary muds than beaches. Loch Paible bends away with machair on one side, crofts and croftland on the other. It was once freshwater and marsh, a continuation of the existing marshes of the nature reserve. People from the townships south of the loch used to row up it and up the length of the then more extensive Loch nam Feithean, to Goular church. But some time in the relatively recent past the crofters decided to drain freshwater Loch Paible for the purposes of agriculture and they dug or deepened an outlet through sand-dunes to the sea. They had overlooked the possibility of the sea coming in, which it did, turning Loch Paible into a tidal inlet. Now, the former freshwater outlet is a sandy channel, at its mouth more than a hundred yards wide, and the upper loch is just like an estuary, with mid-flats and creeks and peripheral salt-marshes. This saline loch was another type of wildlife habitat, adding variety to the already varied reserve.

On my first April visit, I came up from the sea, following the reserve boundary along the central channel of lower Loch Paible, lingering by deep sea pools, thinking that sea trout must surely run here, flushing several greenshanks and scores of curlew from the soft channel-side sands. When I turned with the channel around a narrow cut through sand-dunes and had my first view of the upper part of the loch, I was delighted with it. Ahead were mud-flats piping with waders, ending a mile to the north in a fringe of reeds against sky. On my left was a bay of salt-marsh, dark green and broken up by creeks and pools. A dozen shelduck were moving about on the marsh. They would stay to nest in rabbit holes in the nearby sand-dunes, the nearest thing to hills on the reserve. This was to be my estuary in the coming season, and, though small, it more than compensated me for Ynys-hir and the Welsh estuary which – was it a fortnight ago? – I had been so reluctant to leave.

Like their neighbours in Hougharry, the Balranald crofters had also chosen this first of April to begin their ploughing and sowing. For the first time this year the ploughs were out again and a dozen tractors were turning green land brown on the slopes above Loch Paible. It was a busy, noisy scene. The tractors ground up and down, collies chased and barked after rabbits in the sand-dune warrens, occasionally one ploughman would beckon and shout to another over the din of his tractor. Behind the ploughs paced the sowers, heavy grain bags across their chests, making sweeping gestures with their arms. All the sowers used the same pace-and-throw rhythm, and in broadcasting the grain they did not pivot the arm from the shoulder, but made an underhand armstroke, scattering grain forwards with a wrist flick as if opening a fan.

Ploughers and sowers moved under a sky filled with birds. Gulls in thousands had come from the shore to follow the ploughs; the smaller black-headed and common gulls most numerous and persistent, feeding so close to the plough share that they were in danger of being trapped by the new furrow as it turned. Bigger gulls, herring gulls and black-backs, hung back from the action and harried the smaller species. Their combined screaming almost hid the noise of the tractor engines. The gulls had gathered to easy feeding; other birds were circling and calling just as insistently because their nesting grounds were being disturbed. Redshanks and oystercatchers were shrilly distressed, but the most numerous breeding wader of the machair is the lapwing and they were beating and wailing over the ploughs and men, almost as many of them as gulls, or skylarks of the morning.

Hardly a peaceful scene but I surveyed it all interestedly over a lunchtime sandwich, then walked the damp pasture between salt-marsh and ploughland, following the curve of Loch Paible's shore. Now disturbed lapwings gathered over me like a cloud of big flies, diving close to my head and flinging themselves away, making loud percussive thrumming noises with their wings. The lapwing's is a reedy, plaintive cry, giving the impression of heartbreak. Disturbed redshanks seemed to be singing, hovering as they did so, just as skylarks will sometimes hover and sing when flushed from their nests. Oystercatchers, sturdier birds, sounded downright angry.

The sowers broke rhythm to wave, and one ploughman stopped his tractor at the end of a furrow and came over the machair towards me. His greeting was original.

'I don't know you,' he said.

This was my first meeting with Lachlan Alec Fergusson, crofter and township clerk for Balranald. The clerks are crofters, elected by the men of the township from among themselves. A clerkship lasts for three years, and, though unsalaried, the position entails consid-

erable responsibility. The clerk performs all the township's sec-
retarial work, acts as a mediator of greivances and news, and is the
principal spokesman. If anyone has anything to ask of a township,
involving change in current or traditional practice, he puts the matter to the clerk who gathers opinion, possibly at one of the
township's regular meetings. Since any decision must be unanimous to be carried, every crofter in the township must be consulted. It is the clerk's responsibility to make the final decision
known. Such a system of local politics is only possible where people
live in viable communities.

Fergusson pointed out his house, yet another modern-style
bungalow near the main road. Among the older outbuildings was a
large shiny caravan, conspicuous against hen-houses, tumble-down
barns and the usual litter of derelict farm machinery. Fergusson had
introduced the caravan so that he could accommodate summer
holidaymakers and it had proved to be fairly popular. Already he
had many bookings for the coming year, some of them by people
who had used the caravan before. He talked of his regular visitors as
friends; obviously he looked forward to their arrivals, not only because of financial advantage to himself but because people were
company, in his words, 'Children and all, they make the old place a
bit cheerful.' Possibly because of the nature reserve, many or most
of the caravan users were birdwatchers and they had made Fergusson himself more aware of the birdlife around him. He told me that
if he noticed lapwings' nests on the ground while he ploughed, he
liked to move them to safety, either onto land already ploughed or
somewhere on the pasture among rocks or soft places where tractors were unlikely to go.

There was a gentleness in Fergusson which went with his wide
childlike blue eyes and his quiet island diction. It wasn't difficult,
although he was a large-framed man, to imagine him stopping the
tractor in mid-furrow, bending to lapwing's eggs in the grass and
admiring them for a minute before lifting eggs, nest lining and all,
onto his big hand. A lapwing might sit with comfort and confidence
in Fergusson's palm. Then he would patiently carry the nest to one
side of his tractor path, dig a hole in the ground with his boot heel
and replace the eggs as carefully as he had lifted them. When he had
moved a nest, he liked to mark its new position with a distinctive

stone (there are no sticks on the machair) and watch the parent bird come back to it. As the days went by he would keep an eye on the spot to see if the bird was still sitting and it gave him pleasure if he saw evidence that his nest had produced its full complement of chicks. Four empty eggshells in a nest scrape indicated a successful hatching and he always assumed that small chicks in the immediate area came from 'his' nest. Fergusson had a proprietary feeling for the birds which nested on his land: they were birds free in the wind and the property of no one, but if they nested on his strip of plough-ing, then their growing demanded his protection, just like the growing of his corn.

Fergusson said that once, while he was ploughing, he came across a wader's nest with seven eggs in it. He knew that no wader usually

lays more than four and after moving the nest he watched it with special attention. A snipe came darting back and a few minutes later was joined by a redshank. Two species of wader using one nest scrape; had I ever heard of such a thing?

There was still no cloud in all the sky and now the island seemed full of welcomes. When I left Fergusson and walked on below the ploughlands, other crofters waved and I felt assessed by Balranald township, officially approved by their spokesman.

A track led me between salt-marshes at the head of Loch Paible and a reed-bed crossing a clear-flowing freshwater channel. This must be where the southern part of the reserve's main marshland drains to the sea. Reeds always seem to thrive where saltwater meets fresh and this Balranald reed-bed now rustled to itself in a light breeze. They are intriguing, reed-beds, as if they are hiding something which can only be talked about in a whisper. These reeds had no heads, all must have been stripped off by winter gales. The bed looked thin, many reeds were broken, but the sun was warm on their yellow stems and I could almost believe winter over.

On past the reed-beds and under the walls of Balranald House garden; the house was large by island standards, but square and with walls covered by unpainted harling. It looked durable, unpretentious and a thorn bush grew just outside the front windows. It must once have been part of a hedge, but now this thorn stood alone, and with its thick trunk bent to a right angle by the wind, it looked incredibly ancient.

House and thorn had once been the property of the Ronalds of Clan Macdonald, but both clan and estate had been dispersed and the present owner was a Mrs Pollen who came here only on holiday from London. Tree sparrows nested in the garden walls, but I saw none – perhaps they had gone with other tradition. A pair of collared doves sat on the rim of an unsmoking chimney and these colonisers from the Continent seemed symbolic of change.

Loch nam Feithean was the hub of the marsh and indeed the whole nature reserve; on this first visit I had no idea of just how complicated and extensive its surround of marshland was. I unrolled the map and spread it on a rock near the gateway to Balranald House. It was little help; according to the map, everything between Balranald and Hougharry was either marsh or unwalkable water.

Crouching there, peering at the map and trying to relate it to the landscape, I found it difficult to appreciate that just below, in a hidden shallow trough between the fields of Balranald and its dry-looking machairs, was one of the most important wetlands in Britain, famous for its flora and birds. The land looked no more promising than any fold of neglected pasture. But as I left Balranald House and picked my way across the wet fields, I began to get a truer impression of the marsh.

The birds were immediately evident. That there should be more breeding lapwings, oystercatchers and redshanks than by Loch Paible was hardly credible, but there were far more here. They came out of the peat bogs, like midges after an August shower; they circled, dived, piped, trilled, wept, complained, were a wonder to be heard and seen and a distressing distraction from the business of picking a dry route. A flock of golden plovers, hundreds of them, added their noise, and near my feet ran smaller waders, ringed plovers and dunlins. Whether all these birds were setting up breeding territories or merely resting on migration I couldn't tell; but I had never before seen so many waders together in any freshwater habitat.

What an ideal habitat it was, for waders and indeed any wetland birds. No ordinary pasture, but a mosaic of peat bogs and pools, all sizes and shapes of quagmire and open water contained by ridges and knolls of rock, rushes, rough grass and short heather. An enormous range of bird species could find feeding or breeding conditions to suit their separate requirements here.

If the Balranald marshes seemed a wetland birds' paradise, Loch nam Feithean looked even more promising. I saw it in its entirety for the first time from the south-east, and at this angle it is a flat water in a flat landscape, everything horizontal except Goular church on its knoll above the opposite shore. Beds of emergent vegetation, dead and flattened now in winter condition, would be a colourful scented tangle by early June. Among the vegetation and the pasture of the extraordinarily indented shore were isolated areas of open water; and additional pools, some of them large, glinted among marshes stretching away to the west. There, the section of the marsh penetrating Hougharry's machair is excluded from grazing animals and in the late afternoon sunlight its dead, lengthy vegetation was a wilderness background of yellows, reds, russets.

Wildfowl thronged on Loch nam Feithean. Shrilling waders escorted me between rocks, round the treacherously undefined edge of a pool to a knoll of green turf on the shore. Fifty teal up-ended in the shallows. They are my favourite among all wildfowl, the little teal; smallest of British duck species, adapted to secretive feeding up creeks and under overhanging vegetation. They are pert, lively, never still. They don't quack like plebeian mallard, or whistle romantically like a flighting wigeon, but chirrup softly, like waterside grasshoppers or water-singing crickets.

I was unaware of the presence of geese until an unmistakable resonant honk drew my attention to another grassy knoll on the end of a long peninsula. A score of greylags fed across the knoll just like a flock of sheep and there were more geese, perhaps many more, hidden between the knoll and the shore.

More ducks began to appear; what had seemed a beautiful but empty width of water was now busy with fowl. Mallards, gaudy shovellers, silverily calling dabchicks, six gadwall keeping close together. Tufted duck and golden-eyes in a mixed flock sailing into sight around a bend in the loch, a pair of pochards. Dabblers, geese,

Teal

diving ducks and grebes: what a varied loch it must be, to provide for them all. Wildfowl splashes and calls blended with the clear tones of waders and a heron hunched in the rushes called once, harshly, before taking to slow flight across a sky now reddening towards evening.

Evening: the wildfowl were becoming lively, crofters coming home from their ploughing. Tractors from Hougharry machair went in file beyond the edge of the marshes, then disappeared behind Goular church. Most continued out of sight behind a rise in the field to the township. One tractor separated from the rest. Iain and Murdo, father and son Macdonald, were going home to The Glebe. How natural it seemed, for members of the same family to work together, or, for that matter, members of an entire community. It must demand a great deal of co-operation and accepted interdependence to sustain communal agriculture such as this. What common impulse had taken all the crofters of two townships out that morning to begin ploughing? A precise predetermined date, the first fine day in April; or did they all respond simultaneously and in exactly the same way, to a certain rise in temperature, angle of the sun? Parallels with social insects and colonies of plants occurred to me. The thought of flowers made me laugh to myself – imagine big Lachlan Fergusson opening like a daisy flower to the sun. No, crofters were anything but flowerlike, but all the same they did live more naturally than other people these days, even farmers. Their actions and impulses were in comparatively direct response to conditions of wind, sun, rain, season.

Something of the harmony evident at Ynys-hir was at work also in Uist: Fergusson protecting his lapwings, these marshes curving in such a pleasing way around Goular church, Loch nam Feithean reflecting the machair with its strips of new ploughing; the gull over the furrows, the lapwing crying over the crofter – they were all symbols of a harmony which gave landscapes like these their health and aesthetic attractiveness. For me the glimpse of a man/landscape concord was more satisfying here than in Wales. On the Welsh coast it could only happen at night, with mankind at rest and conflict obscured by darkness. In Uist the harmony existed in daylight, while men were out working in their fields.

I found my way round the edge of the marshes to a road without any difficulty and walked with Loch nam Feitean reflecting sunset and Goular church in silhouette against a still cloudless sky. Lapwings even now were calling and flailing over fields on each side of the road. It was enough for one day. But 1 April wasn't quite finished with me. Cameron's house door opened and the man himself appeared, beckoning. I went up his path and into his house which still stank and was squalid, but was slightly less repulsive than yesterday. He poured me a dram from a whisky bottle, a golden, generous measure. The effect of the spirit on an empty stomach was immediate. I almost liked Cameron's hairy, filthy old visage. On the table mouldy with crumbs he had placed for me the key to the RSPB's cottage and a gift of a bowlful of eggs. Strong drink and an excess of neighbourliness rendered me speechless. When Cameron growled, 'Ye'll find ye're chemical toilet-thing, in the hoose', my cup of happiness, as they say, overflowed.

After its April-fool sunshiny start, the month turned cold and wet. There were days of gales with ferocious showers of hail and snow, when I languished in the caravan and wondered when anybody did any work in such a climate. Under the bed were a dozen metal signs, of fingerpost design, with 'Balranald Nature Reserve' written large on them, and the RSPB's avocet symbol all very attractive in black and white against blue. It would soon be Easter weekend, bank-holidaying birdwatchers would be coming off the ferry and if the signs weren't up they'd be searching all over the island for the reserve.

One morning the gale was without rain or snow, so I put the signs into the back of the van and set out to position them. A hammer and a handful of old staples in the kitchen cupboard comprised the reserve's total stock of tools. With these one sign was attached to a fencepost below The Glebe, pointing the way to Goular. I walloped the staples home, refusing to think about how to get them out again in six months' time. While I worked, someone watched from the sitting-room window of The Glebe: Murdo was watching me, through binoculars. I waved, and he waved back, unabashedly. On then, to the next place for a sign, thinking it was all right for some; these hard-done-by crofters rarely went outside in wind or rain except perhaps once a day, in tractors, to feed the cattle.

Savagely I tried to staple the next sign to its fencepost but struck too hard and the rain-softened post disintegrated. The fenceposts to either side were in a similar condition and that was a problem, since if the next post to the right were used birdwatchers would turn in to the Presbyterian church car-park, and next to the left would have them at Lachie Fergusson's front door, banging and asking for the warden. My visitors must be directed down the road between the two buildings – but where in all this treeless island could a sign be nailed? The fence twanged in the gale and wagged its broken posts. Most of the fence was kept dubiously upright by string and nylon twine, an ingenious agricultural darning. I might take a hint from the crofters and also use string. The RSPB's range of hardware at Balranald didn't run to string, so I untied one of my boots and used the lace. Resourceful people, we wardens. Turning the van to drive away I glanced in the mirror and saw that the wind's fingers had already loosened the bootlace and the sign was now pointing vertically, at the sky. Oh well, the sky is the right place for birds, after all.

The last sign erected was just outside a croft-house, by a fork in the road through Hougharry. There was no sign of life at the house until I had finished stapling the sign, when at the last hammer stroke a small black collie came hurtling round the house corner, cleared the fence in a bound, made a rush with its fangs bared and took a neat piece out of my trousers just below the knee. It turned and came at me again, and this time I beat it off with my hammer. Wary now, it made a lightning half-circle and rushed in from the rear. It was as silent and sharp-toothed as a shark, as difficult to deter. Still the croft-house was empty, either the owners were not in or, more likely, they were in and watching without showing themselves – a good talking point at the next ceilidh. At its third attack I took a desperate kick at the dog and caught it square in the ribs.

The dog rolled into a ditch and my boot minus its lace flew over the roadside fence. As the dog struggled out of the ditch I made a one-booted run for the van, reached it with a muzzle inches away from my stockinged heel and dived in. I accelerated through the township with the dog snapping at the van tyres; would every simple job be as farcical as this?

While the weather was so unsettled, it seemed a good time to do some preparatory work on the cottage and remove Cameron's offending old barn. The cottage hadn't been lived in for years and was in a dreadful state. From outside it looked ruinous, ready to crumble into the rough grass of the machair-edge pasture. It was absurdly small, one tiny room to each side of a central door, and low, the eaves of the roof about 4ft from the ground. The roof had originally been turf, but had been replaced by cheap asbestos slates. The job had been botched, the timbers had rotted, the whole roof sagged and many of the slates were missing. The most ludicrous thing of all was a disproportionately tall and strongly built chimney, sticking out of the middle of the roof like a flagpole. If it hadn't been for that chimney the cottage could easily have been missed, passed by as a heap of stones at the trackside. This, of course, had been the whole principle of the original design, so that weather would flow over it and round it as if it were some stone-heap or moorland outcrop. There were no foundations at all and originally there would have been no chimney; the present chimney and pot had been added recently by someone with no sense of proportion or design.

To enter the house was like crawling into a cave. On the left was the living-room, which had a low wooden ceiling and a huge rusty stove in the middle of the floor. The walls were bare stone and they weren't just damp, they dripped. Under each of the two minute windows was an area of green mould with a pattern of snail tracks; and, though the walls were 3ft thick, it was possible to see light through cracks around the windows and under the eaves. Rats and mice had free passage through holes at the base of the walls, and woodlice clustered in every corner. The other room was slightly better because wood panelling hid the horror of the walls.

To convert this into a combined warden's house and reserve reception would involve an initial stripping down; the rotten ratgnawn woodwork would have to be removed and the stone cleaned. No construction could begin until the place was clean and made weatherproof. As it was, being in there for more than a few minutes was unendurable. Feeling like one of those trapped, dried-up butterflies on the window-sill, my instinct was to beat my way outside, out of the darkness and cobwebs into clean air and light. Chilly though the winds were, it seemed colder inside than outside the cottage.

Cameron's barn was a simple lean-to construction of timber and tin, against the gable of the cottage. It was already partly collapsed, some of the corrugated tin having rusted away and the timber supports being rotted and broken. There was barely room to stand up inside; built low, it had become lower as the floor of cattle dung and straw had risen. Cameron had never cleaned it; when it sheltered cattle they must have wallowed belly-deep in liquid, but now the floor was set hard as stone, level except where tunnelled by rats. With the cottage beside it, the barn was now nothing but a sanctuary for rats and mice.

I was in the barn one day, despairingly contemplating the filth and dereliction, when Cameron sidled in behind me. He accepted one of my cigarettes, sat on a fallen timber and told me something of the history of the cottage. He had been born there, incredibly had lived in the tiny building with his parents and a brother. The brother predictably had succumbed to TB in his teens, but Cameron had lived there for twenty years before the Department of Agriculture had built the house in which he now lived. When his parents had died, Cameron married and stayed on at Goular, crofting, doing odd jobs for the DAFS, including some marsh drainage and maintenance of the church cemetery. The cottage was used as a byre, then sold to an English couple who made it what it now was. But they rarely came, and when the RSPB showed interest in the cottage as a place to house their warden, the English people were pleased to sell it. Cameron had shared the barn with the crofting family who lived in the house behind, now a ruin. When that family moved on and Mrs Cameron died, Cameron stopped keeping cattle and had no further use for the barn.

'It's great timber though – ye canna waste all that wood, can ye? Ye'll have nae use for it, I doot. But I tell ye what, if ye'll bring it

Cottages at Vallay, with the beach behind

across tae me after ye've knocked it doon, I'll use it fine. It'll sort of take it aff ye're hands.'

I was anxious to get on well with Cameron, but not sufficiently to allow him to sell his foul old barn to the RSPB, then receive the wood at my hands. By luck, a satisfactory tactful solution was reached. Rather than that he in his infirmity should tussle with the wood, I would break it all up and carry across the occasional box of firewood kindlings. I could thus preserve dignity by keeping the sawn up timber in my own woodpile, and be credited with some generosity by carrying some for my needy neighbour; also, we both knew perfectly well that Cameron would steal wood from my woodpile. This was precisely what happened and both houses in Goular kept a fire during cool evenings that spring.

The RSPB's tool supply consisted of half a dozen rusty staples, a light joiner's hammer with a fractured handle, one bootlace and a packet of perished rubber bands. More tools were to arrive with furniture and hardware from Edinburgh in May; meanwhile, one or two simple items were required. A spade, crowbar and a cold chisel would suffice, and, though unaware of what shops existed on the island, I assumed that crofters would have somewhere to buy simple essentials like these.

It was 15 miles to Lochmaddy. Here, in the island's only town (of about two hundred inhabitants) was a tobacconist's giftshop which opened only from June to September, a post office, a bank and a general grocery. The tools required might possibly be kept between wellington boots and dried peas. The woman in front of me in the shop delivered a stream of Gaelic ending with, 'one loaf, one tub of margarine and a pound of jelly-babies'. She got what she wanted, but my polite request for 'one spade, one crowbar, one cold chisel', was met with blank incomprehension.

What is Gaelic for crowbar? I tried sign language, making digging, chiselling and wrenching gestures. The woman assistant blenched, gave a frightened smile and said, 'If you'd chust wait a minute, I'll fetch the manager to see you.' The manager arrived, purposefully as if expecting trouble. 'What is it you're after?' he asked, aggressively. This time I explained in clear and simple English the purpose for the tools. The manager was silent for a second or two, then he laid his knuckles on the counter, leaned over and whispered confidentially, 'You don't buy those things, laddie. You borrow them.' It was my first instruction in community living. I bought a boxful of convenience foodstuffs from the shop's adequate stock and left, thinking that for tools, I'd have to go and see the Macdonalds at The Glebe.

The Glebe menfolk were out, but Mary was in as usual, doing one of her twice-weekly bakings. By now I was used to the island custom of walking into a house unbidden and taking a chair. Mary moved between bread oven and table. The kitchen was warm and it was soothing to sit there, unspeaking, just watching Mary.

Most of the island croft wives do a certain amount of baking on their peat-burning kitchen ranges. Peat is free fuel, the ranges are lit all day and night, winter and summer, for cooking and water heating. Baking is an economy and another incentive is the deplorably stale state of bought bread which takes three days to travel from bakeries in Inverness. Rather than rely on this bread from shops and vans, many island women bake scones. Not the rich scone which is eaten at afternoon tea in England, but a scone which is a bread substitute, made with flour and oatmeal, salt water and baking soda. Island scones were no more nourishing than bought bread, but when freshly baked they tasted better.

Mary was a youthful woman, plump, tall, with a brisk manner, and the skin of her face was healthily ruddy, though lined. But her hands were those of an old woman, thick in the palm, large-jointed, heavily veined. They didn't look as though they should belong to the rest of the woman at all, those firm rounded forearms, the capable shoulders. But they worked well enough, those hands of Mary's. They took a double grasp of flour from the bag and dunked it without measurement into the mixing bowl. A good palmful of salt, a generous handful of baking soda, a casual slosh of milk from a tall jug. This was the only home ingredient, the milk from the cow. Fresh or soured the Macdonalds used it only in baking; they never drank it neat, and in tea or coffee they preferred dried powdered milk or evaporated milk from a tin. The milk Mary used in her scones looked creamless and faintly green. She gave this a whisk or two with a spoon, then turned the dough onto a board, to be patted into a foot-square flat rectangle.

This patting was the important thing; Mary did it quickly, lightly; it was astonishing to see those aged knotted hands move so lightly and fast. In seconds she had a smooth dough which looked ready to rise – as though left to itself it would turn into scones without further cooking. A few decisive strokes with a sharp bread knife – again, no hesitation at all, no measuring – and in the same smooth movement the individual scones were flipped onto a baking tin. By the time one batch was ready, the last batch was baked. Mary opened the oven door and withdrew one sheet of browned scones, replacing it with the sheet of dough: a rapid rhythmical baking and in this way Mary could turn out two or three dozen scones in an hour.

As Mary worked, she told me about the bakings she had done as a girl. Then, there were no grocers' vans to the door with bread and cakes, nor was it easy to buy flour. You used your own oatmeal, stone ground or threshed, and your baking took all of one day, twice a week. Little bread was made, it was mainly bannocks, scones and oatcakes, unleavened but better, Mary said, than these things made with bought flour and soda; more solid — a few scones with crowdie, potatoes, eggs fresh from the hen, maybe a fish or a rabbit, a glass of milk warm from the cow. That made a proper meal. 'People wass stronger then,' said Mary. 'They did more work and they wass eating stronger foods.' Major domestic tasks like baking or washing occupied whole long days and all the women of the household joined in. Mother worked with and organised her daughters; grandmother looked after the babies, tending to them and keeping them out of harm's way. 'People worked more together then,' said Mary, lugging out the meal for the first batch of oatcakes.

They were good for me, these occasions when I sat in Mary's kitchen. She wasn't a garrulous woman but told me a lot of casual island gossip, and township history, past and present customs and mores. It was better than history from books, giving me a working knowledge of the community. History as learned from Mary wasn't finished, it was a living continuity with the present.

Tools supplied, renovations must begin with demolition, a complete annihilation of Cameron's barn, and a clearing out of decayed woodwork in the cottage itself. This suited me. Not being a DIY enthusiast, constructive carpentry or building is mostly beyond me, but I do enjoy useful destruction.

It was too wet and windy to work on the barn, so I began with the inside of the cottage. Before paints and building materials arrived from Edinburgh little improvement could be made to the room which was to be the warden's living quarters. The stove was ancient and ruinous but necessary to keep me warm while working, and windows couldn't be replaced without proper timbers and cement. The room could be tidied only in a superficial, temporary way, warmed by a fire in the stove, and because the windows were jammed shut, the door must be opened to dispel years of staleness and stagnancy.

I cleared out the stove, set match to newspaper in the rust-eaten grate, and fed the flames with pieces of a broken up worm-holed chair. The cottage immediately filled with smoke. With the door wide open to the machair, it was just possible to endure the smoke and work indoors, and it was warmer to do this than to have no fire at all. I fed more pieces of chair into the stove and, with stinging eyes and rasping throat, began demolitions in the other room.

Here, there was more to occupy me. Wooden panelling on walls and wooden ceiling were both utterly decayed and would have to go. I swung my crowbar at the wall. The wood was soft as damp cardboard; it fell and flaked away, leaving nails in the mortar behind. Panel after panel, the pieces of worthless wood were stacked in the other room as fuel for the stove. It really was most satisfying.

Behind the old panels was not stone, but a layer of unidentifiable substance which might have been mortar or plaster originally laid over the gappy stone of the walls. Now, whatever it was had the texture of earthy sand, was blackened by peat-smoke, and stank of rats and mice. When the panelling came away this stuff stayed on the wall and it was like a cross-section through a rat's castle; all the runs and old nests and dormitories were visible. For the present there were no rats or mice, only thousands of woodlice in little scuttling clusters, innumerable beetles, centipedes, millipedes and snails. This cottage in its state of decay was possibly as important a sanctuary for invertebrate life as the marshes outside were for their birds.

Birds were my business, not insects, so I took a spade and quite literally dug out the walls. Hundredweights of this foul peat-smoke and rat deposit were bagged up and dumped outside at a safe distance from the cottage. The walls were black, damp, with gaps inches in diameter through their 3ft thickness. The demolition took most of three days – filthy, mindless sort of work, but satisfying. It laid bare the essential structure of the cottage. An intimidating prospect, to turn these two empty, draughty rooms into a warden's living accommodation and an office/information area fit for the reception of reserve visitors.

The first day that the weather relented enough to allow me to work on the barn happened to be a Sunday. The Highlanders'

Creel fishing boats at Lochmaddy

Sabbath was sacred, but I assumed that restrictions wouldn't apply to me. Any way, I was impatient and in such unsettled weather anxious to take advantage of any day without wind and rain.

To minimise any offence, work was delayed until mid-morning. Machair and township were deserted, even the weather seemed to be observing the Sabbath, wind and rain taking a rest and allowing high white clouds to pass reverentially across bluest sky.

I stood on the roof of the barn and started pulling old nails out of the iron sheets with the claw-hammer. Lapwings rose in protest from their nests on the machair fields, the crows circled the gable of Goular church. Some of the nails were welded by rust to the roof sheets, and to these I took the crowbar, hammering and wrenching until the nails drew free. Twenty nails to the sheet, twenty sheets to the roof, this job was going to take all day. One sheet fell over the side of the barn with a crash and a scattering of rusty fragments.

Getting to work on the second sheet, I warmed to it and forgot about Hougharry and the Sabbath. Feeling happier in the work, I whistled and gave short bursts of song. After all, it was spring, and weren't the skylarks out there busily nest-building and singing? The second sheet came off and dropped on top of the first. A door slammed and Cameron stalked from his gate down the track towards me. He was moving with unusual speed and purpose. I stood to face him, dangling the crowbar guiltily in one hand.

'Chust wait,' Cameron said, while still walking. 'Chust you wait till the church commissioners hear about this!' His face quivered, his voice was a gibber with a Highland accent. Caught like a naughty schoolboy in the act, I waited for him to calm down.

'You can't – we don't – it isn't right, to do that, on a Sunday.' In Hougharry ears in a dozen houses pricked to listen. Was it any use, to pretend ignorance?

'I am sorry, Mr Cameron. Of course I didn't think, you'll have to excuse me for not being used to your ways. If you think that to work might offend anybody then I'll stop, immediately.'

Cameron calmed, became apologetic. 'It's not me that minds, you understand, it's what others might think.' He gave a furtive glance towards the village. 'You might give Goular a bad name. The church commissioners, if they heard . . . .'

Cameron, now quite amiable, began to tell me about Sunday on Uist. It wasn't long ago, he said, since people separated the cock from the hens on Saturday night, the ploughshare had to be lifted from the ground at the end of the furrow, the spade laid on its side. Such rigid Sabbatarianism was rare nowadays, he admitted, but still no islander would do work of any kind on Sunday, and some families would stay indoors except to go to the kirk, once for morning service and again in the evening. Reading, other than the Gaelic Bible, listening to or watching other than religious programmes on radio or TV, were disapproved rather than condemned. Only a few, now, he said wistfully as if he regretted the change, refused to do any household chores including lighting fires, cooking, washing of dishes. Principles were relaxing and some people on very fine Sundays had even started taking recreational walks; but still any noisy, conspicuous activity was to be avoided. Demolishing old iron barns was definitely out.

Cameron stayed chatting for a while, then puffing one of my cigarettes wandered off back to his house. Hougharry slept on in the morning sunshine. How many of its people had witnessed my ticking off? There was an air of self-righteousness about the quiet of the morning and I subdued a rising childish rebelliousness.

I would not work on the barn, risk the wrath of the church commissioners, whoever they may be, whatever their powers. But neither would I stay indoors and waste a glorious day like this in watching my neighbour for signs of outrage, or broodily review the sins of the world. A day of rest was acceptable but not a day of utter joylessness. In a few minutes I had flask and sandwiches made, and set out towards the machair for a Sabbath in the sun.

Any slight resentment was soon dispersed by the walking, the sun, the infinite smiling distances of sky and sea. All was benign, it just had to be a happy, relaxed day. So much better than working on that wretched barn, to be here freely walking the lowtide sands of Traigh Iar. The machair was deserted, there was no one visible on miles of dazzling sand. In future, I'd take advantage of every Sunday, to census or merely watch the birds on the reserve while they were undisturbed by crofters at work.

Day and place were entirely mine. My bare feet squeaked in the soft sand and made shallow imprints where the sand was hard, wandering from this object to that along the tide-line, weaving among rock pools of the lower shore. I examined the carcase of a porpoise and a thick worm-riddled section of ship's timber, and sorted among nets and plastic flotsam for anything which might be of use. Sandhoppers seethed in a bank of decaying seaweed, but nearer the sea the sands were hard, cool and clean. It was a surface for little waders to run on, purely piping. Colours were sharp and the sea crisped lightly to a rim of thin foam and bubbles. When a small breeze played in from the sea it was fresh, salty, invigorating.

No sense of time, no urgency about anything, wandering alone and forever somewhere beyond the edge of the known world. At the mouth of Loch Paible there was a broad issue of sea-going freshwater between me and the next southward sweep of sand. That was Benbecula in the distance, houses of the military base and town of Balivanich quivering like a mirage. An inverted white cone of concrete water-tower rose near Benbecula airport and various buildings associated with MOD rocket ranges lined the shore. There was a warring humanity in that direction. I preferred the peaceful estuary with its waters ebbing steadily, its sands marked by worm casts, cockle beds and the footprints of many birds.

On all the flat treeless machair of the bird reserve there are not many sheltered suntraps, but there was a hollow in the dunes at the mouth of Paible and many times that season I was to come to it after

Whimbrel

walking the western beaches, fit myself into its green chair-like recess and relax with flask and sandwiches and the glorious view to the south. If there is sun, it strikes directly into the face of the dunes and cool onshore winds are baffled by a ridge of marram. It is also the most distant point on the reserve from Goular, the RSPB cottage and visiting birdwatchers, and it provided me with seclusion without my having to leave the reserve. A good place to come, on a fine Sunday, for an outdoor lunch and a sleepy birdwatch over the mouth of the inlet, a stretch among the short-stemmed daisies and perhaps the luxury of a brief daytime doze. Marram spikes rattling in a slight breeze; curlew and greenshank calls mingling with ringed plover pipings from the sea pools; the everlasting duet of seagulls and sea; sun intense and heavy on closing eyelids.

A woman's voice said my name. Clear, English, part of a dream, but there was a woman standing in the marram at the edge of my sun hollow, looking down at me and smiling.

'You are Philip Coxon, aren't you, the new bird warden at Goular? I'm Patricia Pollen, from Balranald House. I'm sorry to wake you but I came on you so suddenly. Shall I go away and leave you in peace?'

She stepped lightly over the rim of the dune and settled herself beside me on the grass.

'I must say you have taste in places to escape to, for the Sabbath. My God, you couldn't do much better, could you, than this?'

My first impression was of a girl, a teenager, with slight figure made boyish by shooting jacket, jeans and wellington boots. Her movement too was light and youthful; but her voice had the assurance of maturity and as she sat with her back to me, staring out to sea, grey showed in the wind-tangled black of her hair. The face that turned to me with a friendly but mocking smile was thin, small-featured, again youthful, but there were weather or laughter wrinkles around the eyes. In her mid-forties, Patricia Pollen, like many of her type and class, had more vitality than most girls in their teens. Her manner was disingenuous. There was simple friendliness in her smile.

Patricia was wearing gardening gloves, an old battered pair which didn't quite accord with her other fairly conventional clothing. The fingers of the gloves were lumpish and stiff and she must surely find it difficult, wearing them and focusing the expensive, finely adjusting binoculars which were slung round her neck. She said with a laugh that she'd been gardening at Balranald House – she was 'really fearfully keen on getting the old garden back into shape' – when she'd seen me on the skyline, crossing the dunes. Guessing who I was – who else could it be, walking from Goular to Paible on a Sunday? – she had decided to come and introduce herself.

'I thought you must be awfully diligent, out doing a bird count or something on a Sunday. Then I find you fast asleep in a sand-dune!'

True to type, however, Patricia could be peremptory, and, having tracked me down, she had no intention of allowing me to doze away my Sunday afternoon. She wanted to learn about birds, she announced. Damn silly to be surrounded by the things and not know their names. Please would I teach her, starting now. The disarming smile again. 'Then when we've had enough I'll give you tea back at the house.'

There was no better way to spend a fine afternoon. Many crofters were rewarding, interesting people, but after almost a month on the island, I needed a change.

Bar-tailed godwit

We began with the birds of the estuary mouth immediately below us. No better place than the mouth of Loch Paible, for a lesson on the identification of British waders. Patricia knew lapwings and she knew curlews. Now she could learn that some of the birds which had perplexed her were golden plovers: dumpy, without the lapwing crest. 'Aren't they dull?' Wait, focus properly on that one at the edge of the flock, see the glints of gold, the fritillary patterning of black, white and brown on its back. And that other one, in more definite breeding plumage with black from breast to underbelly; more subtle than a lapwing's metallic greens and purples.

'It's all a matter of taste,' I insisted, and now it was my turn to be gently mocking.

'Oh, I do love the curlews,' exclaimed Patricia. But they weren't curlews, out there lining the tide's edge. Curlews rarely flocked like that, out in the open; they preferred the more secluded and seaweedy rock pools; and anyway, if she looked closely she would see that these curlew-sized waders were lighter in colour, grey rather than brown, and had straight bills, not the downward curving bills of the curlews. 'Bar-tailed godwits,' I pronounced. 'See how some of their bills even turn up a bit, at the ends. One or two of them are showing red underneath, these are probably immature birds, the adults have deeply red necks and bellies in spring.' I didn't admit to Patricia that godwits were relatively new to me; only since coming to Uist had I been able to learn the finer points of their identification. We watched a flock of thirty moving southwards along the wave's edge, until they lost definition against a glitter of sunlight on wet sand and sea.

'What about these little things? I know there are dunlins and ringed plovers but how anyone tells them apart beats me.' Both species were there, many of each, on the sands and among the shingles of the estuary's main channel. Dunlin, like half-size golden plovers with proportionally longer bills, their call something between a sneeze and a trill. Ringed plovers, squat, pale grey, pied black and white faces, tiny stubby bills and red legs twinkling when they run. No birds are more endearing than ringed plovers with their teddy-bear tubbiness and their softly piping calls. Among the ringed plovers were one or two turnstones, now in tortoiseshell summer plumage, and, unlike plovers and dunlins, preferring to feed among the shingles rather than on the mud and sands. The little waders rested and probed and picked around, moving like clockwork toys. Suddenly they all took flight with one of those inexplicable flock impulses: in a tight flock turning light to dark as underparts, then wings were turned to the sun, more like a swarm of insects than a flock of birds. They moved so quickly and erratically that it was difficult to follow them, then just as suddenly as they had gone, they were back in their places again, on the sand below us.

Ringed plover

'They don't even seem out of breath,' said Patricia, wonderingly. Patricia, like me, was most interested in the wading birds. She was attentive but unenthusiastic when I identified for her the different species of gulls, and pointed out how massive a raven's beak is compared to a crow's. 'If there's nothing to give you a clue to its greater size, and you can't see whether it's grey-patched or all black, you can always tell a raven by its bigger head and the wedge shape of its tail.'

'Oh,' said Patricia. Then, 'What's that?' as a greenshank came calling over the sea pools. Her interest was in Uist, not merely birds, and waders more than any other species are the essence of the Uist landscape. Song-birds and seagulls would be missed if they weren't there, but only waders with their pure wild cries and quick movements, their other-worldliness, can express the atmosphere of estuarine wetland. Big skies over sky-reflecting muds and sands, pools, channels, creeks, salt-marshes; the richness of it despite its apparent desolation; all conveyed by a thousand dunlin drifting mist-like over distant sand-bars, or a single greenshank flighting down a creek.

All the way up Loch Paible we found waders, and stopped again and again to discuss identification and habits. The afternoon stretched timelessly, but the tide came up behind us, pushing us in front of it with the birds, finally edging us aside into the salt-marshes. Just as we left the sands, I heard a call like a golden plover's, but slurred into three syllables even more melodic. We flopped into the wet saltings and focused binoculars on three birds coming together at the head of the tide: grey plovers, not golden, whitish tails and black patched underwings recognisable from memory of illustrations in bird books. They are not rare birds but they were new to Patricia and me, and we watched them until the rising tide drove them out of sight. Then, like a couple of tide-driven waders ourselves, we splashed over salt-marsh to the machair.

Although sharing Patricia's liking for waders, I reserved a great deal of interest for the birds of prey. Falcons, buzzards, owls, eagles, whatever the species and wherever it occurs, from kestrels on high-rise flats in the city to eagles in the remotest Highlands, these raptorial birds instantly dominate attention and introduce a wildness to their setting. We both thrilled when a cock hen harrier lifted from the Balranald reed-beds. From down among the tangle of winter stems and grasses it lifted steeply and curved away, up-flung white wings catching the sunlight. It didn't fly out of sight, but banked down again over the reed tops, wavering over the slightly swaying stems like some huge butterfly.

We were engrossed, as much appreciative of the whole setting of sunlit winter-coloured marshland and sand-dune, ragged marginal croftland, all enhanced by this bird. It flew low and slowly, balancing intricately with long wings and tail, dominating the wind as it seemed to dominate the whole landscape. In the intense, oblique light of late afternoon, the very pale blue of the plumage was emphasised, and as the bird threw itself sideways in a dive down among the reeds, we caught a clear glimpse of startlingly yellow legs and talons.

Patricia must have felt, as I did, that the harrier was almost too beautiful to be real; it was like a principal character in some show which the marshes were putting on for our benefit. As we turned through the gate to Balranald House we were both rather subdued, perhaps awed by the abundance and variety of birdlife we had seen in a short afternoon. Patricia's enthusiasm for a new hobby couldn't have had greater stimulus, and I saw opportunities for study projects and photography. I was as excited as Patricia, although sensible enough to realise that a great deal of my pleasure came from her company and the prospect of having more of it in the near future.

Cock hen harrier

The question of apportioning my time among various commitments now began to bother me. The barn demolition caused no further problems and in fair weather the work was quickly done. Work inside the cottage had gone as far as possible with my present equipment, and I was quite satisfied with progress as far as practical manual tasks were concerned.

It was time to turn my attention to less mundane tasks. At mid-April the birds' breeding season was well underway, time to begin a proper census. Birds have such a short, intense breeding season from April, coming to a climax in the second half of May, tailing off and finishing for most species by the end of June. The waders which were the main group of birds nesting at Balranald, and the flat, unrelievedly open habitat were strange to me. Both would have to be studied thoroughly and a systematic approach to the business devised.

It occurred to me also that my attention had been confined to the 1,500 acres of the bird reserve. Work on the cottage and initial familiarisation with my 'patch' had so far occupied most of my time. Balranald was special, but it was only a small part of an island rich in bird life throughout, and my duties would inevitably extend beyond the boundary of the reserve.

When demolition of the barn was complete, I heard from Edinburgh that furniture for the cottage and tools for its further renovation were due to arrive. The assistant director, Peter Walker, had been gathering things together from hardware shops, builders' yards, timber merchants and auctions, and the Edinburgh office was becoming obstructed by bulky packages labelled 'for Balranald'. As soon as he could arrange to hire a vehicle, probably within the next few days, Peter would himself load up and drive to Uist. He would stay with me for a few days in order to learn something about a reserve and part of Scotland he hadn't yet seen.

The tone of a long memo from Edinburgh telling me all this, and asking for advice on routes and ferry times, was one of anticipated adventure. Peter expected a good time, a holiday from the office. But although I would be pleased to accommodate him and was prepared to share his three-day adventure, the arrival of tools did cause me some concern. Was I expected to carry straight on with work on the cottage and try to prepare an information centre for the coming season? If so, there would be no time for bird censusing or anything else, and this seemed a most undesirable restriction of my role as warden. Relatively new to my post and therefore inclined to be submissive, this question of correct allocation of effort was nevertheless important to me, something to take up with Peter when he arrived.

Peter certainly didn't waste any time over organising his journey to Uist. A telegram arrived, telling me that he would be with me the very next day. Too impatient to wait for advice about ferries, he had chosen to disregard the short crossing from Skye and come instead via Oban to Lochboisdale in South Uist. To travel from Edinburgh by this route would mean less driving for Peter, but after his road journey from Edinburgh to Oban, followed by at least six hours on the ferry, he would be faced with a 50-mile drive up the Uists to Balranald. The least I could do was drive down to Lochboisdale, meet him off the ferry and act as guide/companion on the last part of his journey.

The weather had been fine for about a week, but on the morning of Peter's intended arrival, it broke with sheets of rain on a strong south-westerly wind. By mid-morning the wind had increased to something more severe than a gale, and the rain seemed to take on a deliberate relentless savagery, beating down on the caravan as if it meant to pierce the metal roof. Poor Peter, coming from Oban head-on into this. With flasks of strong coffee and lots of solid sandwiches, I made an early start for Lochboisdale.

This was to be my introduction to the other islands of the southern section of the Outer Hebrides; Benbecula first, then South Uist. The islands are separated by tidal sand-flats, crossable only at low tides before the construction of the present causeway and roads. At one time it must have been a hazardous business, crossing the unstable wastes of north and south fords on foot or horseback. Tidal channels change their courses, the tides are unpredictable in stormy weather, and there were tales of whole parties of people drowned while attempting to get home at night or after gatherings at cattle fairs or ceilidhs. A short end to conviviality, this terrible in-sweeping of the tides.

Benbecula and South Uist were, if anything, more celebrated than North Uist for their scenery and birds, and this necessary journey might have provided a first glimpse of their famous machairs and marshes. In the event, that April drive was a most depressing journey. Everything about that 50 miles was oppressively dreary, and the filthy weather wasn't wholly responsible for my initial reaction of distaste.

The townships of North Uist had seemed peculiarly unattractive, but they were salubrious compared to those of Benbecula and South Uist. Where North Uist settlements were generally bleak and devoid of any evidence of aesthetic sensibility, one could reasonably euphemise them as utilitarian or untidy, whereas every township beyond North Ford was uncompromisingly squalid. There was abandoned machinery of every type, everywhere. Old tractors, cars, lorries, parked and left to rust in passing places by the road, in roadside ditches, in the centre of fields. Almost every croft-house stood at the centre of what looked like a used car lot. Some of the vehicles were skeletons of rust, others more recently abandoned and intact, used as hen-houses or dog-kennels. North Uist had its share of old vehicles on display, but it was freer of the even more unsightly, ephemeral rubbish which cluttered the southern islands. Old mattresses, disintegrating on the grass in the front of houses, and plastic bags spilling domestic refuse, simply dumped at the roadside among naked heaps of bottles and tins. Halfway down South Uist, I felt that I was touring Britain's junkyard.

The townships were undefined, seemingly consisting of unlovely modern bungalows built in a continuous ribbon development on each side of the road. I passed a quarry, a supermarket-style shop which looked like a warehouse, the inevitable petrol pump apparently attended by a bedraggled and savage collie. All the way, I had to fight the steering wheel to keep the van from blowing off the road, and my windscreen wipers could barely cope with the volume of rain. Over the fords, the wind blew even more strongly and at high tide it might be dangerous to attempt to drive over the causeways. The road was narrow, very exposed, and built at no great height above sands which would be racing and raging sea-water when tides were at flow.

It would have been foolish of me to base any lasting opinion on this experience. The weather couldn't have been worse, and the main road bypasses all that is best of Benbecula and South Uist, both of which islands have machair-lands of exceptional loveliness. South Uist has a fine hinterland of mountain country dropping to an uninhabited, almost unvisited coast of moorland and sea cliff in the east. On that first unfortunate visit I had to fight consciously against a growing depression. By the time I reached Lochboisdale I wished that I'd left Peter Walker to make his own way to my caravan.

I expected to meet a sick man off a delayed ferry; but amazingly the ferry was only half an hour late and Peter Walker was in the best of spirits. It had indeed been a rough crossing, the boat occasionally vertical, people reeling about being seasick and a shipment of cattle bellowing in the hold. Peter himself had been exhilarated, not a trace of illness. Between attempts at consoling other passengers, he had spent much of the journey on deck, standing in the shelter of the body of the ship and positively enjoying its movement in the gale. Now, he said, he was hungry, ravenous, having eaten nothing since bacon and egg breakfast on the ferry. I mentioned my flask and sandwiches; perhaps we could pull off the road and eat these? Peter dismissed any suggestion of mere sandwiches; 'Good Lord, man, I said I'm hungry, I've just spent more than six hours on a boat!'

It would have to be the hotel – there is nowhere else to eat – in Lochboisdale. Peter led the way up a steep road to the hotel, a large building dominating pier and township. It has since changed its image, but in those days it was a fishermens' resort, reputedly rather exclusive and expensive. Peter breezed into the 'Anglers' Lounge' and I followed, conscious among elegant furnishings of my rough outdoor clothes, my wellington boots. The bar was empty, the fishermen had all gone fishing in the rain, and the hotel seemed quiet, as if resting. Perhaps an angler's mood had permanently affected the place; it suggested riverbank pipe-lighting, patient selection among tiny artificial flies, and the contemplation of waters.

Peter wasn't at all intimidated. He ordered drinks and a lunch menu, and when the menu came said without looking at it that he'd have trout, grilled, with all the trimmings. Driving down the islands had done nothing for my appetite and I ordered omelette, plain. Relaxed, I began to enjoy this contrast to life in the caravan. I hung my dripping jacket over a chair, eased my legs under the table and

Boats at Lochmaddy

felt my toes warm inside rubber boots. A light steam rose from my knees. Did I smell of Goular, of unwashed clothes, sheep and paraffin? Another gulp of sherry and I ceased to care. Peter, over his third glass of stout, was telling me about the pressure of work at HQ. New reserves to get into shape for the season, protection to organise for rare species, interviews of seasonal staff. Spring was the busiest time of the year at the office; some days the sheer volume of work seemed overwhelming.

I studied him across the table. He didn't look like a man oppressed by office work. More like a cherub out on a treat, round unlined face healthily shining, everything about him plump, easy going, suggestive of a permanent holiday attitude to life. He was ecstatic in his approval of his plateful of trout, creamed potatoes, green peas; and he ate it in large, noisy mouthfuls. There was nothing quiet about Peter. He downed the trout and, hardly pausing for breath, started on a second course, a substantial segment of apple pie with thick custard.

'What about some biscuits and cheese? I hope they've got Stilton.' He was crunching oatcakes while I was still finishing my omelette, and between bites and gulps of scalding coffee, he managed to talk incessantly.

The purpose of this visit was not only to deliver my tools and domestic equipment. All was in the van; we would unload it and forget it. Tools and suchlike were unimportant compared with the real purpose of the visit, which was to tour the islands in search of rare birds. Peter was a relative beginner in birdwatching; his new position with the RSPB made him conscious of his inexperience and he wanted to 'tick off' some 'raries', mainly to impress his colleagues at the office.

'Frank saw a yellow-breasted bunting last week at Insch, and John got a Wilson's phalarope at Joppa sewage outlet. I've got to tick off some raries; what have you got up here?' He leaned forward and spoke confidentially, as if afraid someone might overhear. 'D'you know, I haven't even seen a storm petrel yet. They breed here, don't they? Everybody's seen them. What I really want to see on this trip, if nothing else, is a storm petrel.'

Storm petrels are small sea birds which breed on some of Britain's remote oceanic islands. They are thoroughly pelagic, requiring contact with land only during the breeding season, but they may be carried close to mainland shores by violent storms. Birdwatchers seem to have a special affection for them, probably because they are small and frail. In size and general appearance they are rather like ocean-going house martins, yet always associated with the remotest of places, wildest of weather. They seem small survivors in a big world of storms.

Peter was dismayed to hear that sightings of storm petrels couldn't be guaranteed; nor were there any particularly rare birds currently on the reserve. But he was an inveterate optimist, convinced that there must be some rare birds out here in the islands, and we'd be sure to find them if we devoted enough energy to the search.

Out immediate task was to get back to Balranald with the van load of equipment for the reserve. The gale was still raging outside. It was tempting to linger in the warm hotel lounge, perhaps accept another cup of this excellent coffee. I knew what Balranald was like in the rain and was in no hurry to get back to it; but Peter was now well fed and ready for the next part of his adventure. He paid the bill for our meal while I stared hard at a stuffed salmon in a glass case on the wall, then we were outside again, in the wind and rain. Peter yelled into my car, 'You drive on first and go slowly, keep a look-out for birds. Be sure to stop if you see anything interesting.'

The idea of birdwatching in these conditions was ludicrous and I was simply thankful that the tide was still out as we crossed the fords, the road almost empty of other traffic. We turned off the track at the caravan and parked in floodwater which had accumulated several inches deep since that morning.

The contents of Peter's van were to be stored in the RSPB cottage, and shortly after arriving back we began to unload. As item by item came off the van, it was evident that Peter had either disregarded or somehow misinterpreted my written request for a few strong elementary tools and a minimum of sturdy, simple furniture. Peter handed out a set of four chromium and plastic bar stools from the rear of the van and I packed them away without comment. The cooker was a camper's plaything, far too flimsy and requiring gas cylinders of a type unavailable in Uist. I had asked for a standard Calor cooking top, a simple affair of two burners and a grill, in the knowledge that cylinders could be supplied by a gas agent on the island. Still I said nothing, not wanting to spoil Peter's holiday mood. But when a power drill complete with electric extension cable appeared, I couldn't refrain from pointing out: 'Peter, you know there isn't any electricity, here.'

'Isn't there, but how are you going to have light? It looks pretty dark in there to me.'

'I asked you to bring Tilley lamps. Two, together with methylated spirits, paraffin, and spare mantles.'

'Yes, but I thought you couldn't really mean it. They're so antiquated, nobody buys those things these days. You ought to have electricity, you know; besides, I've got lots of things here . . .'

I tried to keep my voice quiet. 'Would you mind if we just have a look through this stuff before it comes off the van? It may save some of the labour of unloading.' There were four easy chairs, but no bed and no table. A forty-piece dining set complete with cruet and napkin rings, a dozen table-mats. 'I thought you'd like those mats, they've got a bird design on them.' I accepted the dining set and the mats but a few items later expostulated: 'This is a bit much, this electric coffee-bean grinder. Even if there was electricity, where d'you think I'd find coffee beans in Uist? It's tea-bags here, and then only one brand, the cheapest. And what's this thing underneath, another electrical gadget?'

'It's a hairdrier.'

Anger dissolved and I hung on to the back of the van to prevent myself falling into floodwater, weak with laughter. Perfect for Cameron, I thought. 'That's pretty useful, Peter. You didn't happen to think of talcum powder, did you? It could make a lot of difference to the tone of life in Goular.' In mutual hilarity we examined the rest of the load, separated out the few useful items and left the rest in the van to be taken back to Edinburgh. 'Just more litter for some sand-dune. You can take it back and have an auction. Though, wait a minute, on second thoughts I will have that deck-chair.'

Next morning I suggested we walk the reserve, thinking that Peter might want to inspect the RSPB's only holding in the Western Isles; but no, Peter said he'd rather wait until the bad weather blew over, or drive. 'It won't blow over, it'll probably get worse. This is good April weather for Uist.'

So we drove, turning inland by the moorland road. At the head of a rocky bay we stopped to watch two greylag geese and a mute swan feeding in the mud. They were the first birds of any sort we had seen since leaving the croftland and Peter showed signs of impatience. He could see geese and swans in Edinburgh's municipal parks. 'If you'd just walk a bit we might find something,' I cajoled. 'You can't expect the birds to be on view like ducks in a drive-in wildlife park.' Spreading my map, I pointed to a small blue circle like an egg in a nest of brown contours. 'Why don't we climb this hill and find this little loch?'

Peter grumbled, but he got out of the van and we walked together over a rising moor towards the hill. The wind came cold across the flat centre of Uist, but it was a clean wind, tasting of rain and salt. Raindrops flashed in the heather and it seemed I could run the mile across the moor, climb the hill in an effortless minute. But Peter was fat, unfit, already breathless.

'Blue-bottomed peatwarblers,' I yelled. 'Come on.'

'You string of Celtic bones, I'll fire you.' It seemed to take ages, but eventually we reached a cairn of stones at the hilltop and found the loch below in a perfectly bowl-shaped hollow: a dark peaty water like all the moorland lochs, but larger than we had expected because swollen by recent rains. I was captivated by the sheltered seclusion of the spot and its basin-like symmetry. Set in such a complex landscape, loch and hollow seemed an enclosed, separate world. You could come here and sit by the shore, and the winds of the day would never reach you.

Peter's response was less contemplative. 'There's a bird on it,' he announced. We focused binoculars on a movement among flooded rushes at the loch's edge and saw a slim duck-shape for a second. Then the bird dived, leaving ripples and bubbles. A moment later it came up again, not bobbing up like a duck or grebe, but sliding otter-like to the surface, seeming to feel its way through the meniscus. It lay there, low as a shadow, ripples washing over its back.

It was a red-throated diver, a bird typical of Uist as nowhere else, although in fact they breed on moorland water over most of northern Scotland. In the near future I was to see dozens of them around the coast and the inland lochs, but meanwhile it was an uncommon enough sight to excite Peter. He lunged forward and downhill, trying for a clearer view, and disappeared entirely into a bog hole in the heather. One minute he was there, the next he wasn't. The moors

Red-throated diver

have many such traps, where fronds of heather conceal clefts among rocks or holes filled with liquid peat. They make it necessary for any walker always to be aware of his feet.

It was one of the boggy sort that claimed Peter. As he fell he collapsed forwards, face down in the bog, so that for a second he was completely submerged. When he raised his head he was like something from a more lurid legend, a monster emerging black and dripping from the bog.

The diver gave a cackle and flew away towards the sea. Even the loch seemed to shake itself into ripples of laughter. I found it all mildly amusing, if a little slapstick, but less funny by the time I had hauled him out and we were both peat-blackened and wet to the skin.

Peter was shocked and speechless and we simply bundled ourselves down the hill and into the van. Soaked, chilled to the point of numbness and teeth chattering, there was no question of further birdwatching. We drove in an evil-smelling silence by the shortest route back to Balranald.

The day Peter left we took a walk across the southern section of the reserve to the mouth of Loch Paible. He didn't want to go; it was a showery cold day and he wanted to hug the paraffin heater until it was time to drive to the ferry. 'I haven't seen anything,' he groaned. 'Not a single new species.'

In the end he came out with me and we had a bracing walk over the machair. The sun broke through briefly, richly colouring grasses, salt-marsh and sand-flats. At the mouth of the inlet, however, we walked into another shower and it was just then, from the rocks at the southern extremity of the reserve, that a storm petrel fluttered towards us over the sea. Of all the birds in the world, the one he most wanted to see. It came with typical flight, scraping wave crests and skimming down the troughs, deceptively fragile, but in reality perfectly at home out there, at one with wind and water. It passed within a few feet of us, and I could easily pick out the steep brow, down-pointing bill and black petrel's eye. The white feathers of its rump were sharply defined between the smoky grey-black of wings and tail. It was an unsurpassable view of the bird in its element.

Peter missed it, however. His spectacles had misted up and were

Storm petrel

speckled by the shower, and by the time he'd whipped them off and wiped them clear, the storm petrel had gone.

Before Peter finally departed, I asked permission to defer work on the cottage until a first census of the breeding birds had been completed. Since he had failed to bring the tools and materials for the job and I would now have to shop around the island in a time-wasting manner, a refusal was unlikely.

'Do what you like,' he said, surprised. 'I don't care when you do up your cottage.' He offered me some advice. 'Don't take yourself so seriously. Nobody in the office really gives a damn about you, or Balranald, so long as you don't destroy the place. You ought to let yourself go. Enjoy yourself, while you've got the chance.' Sound advice no doubt, and well intentioned, but a career in nature conservation does require a certain amount of dedication to the 'cause', otherwise the demands are too great and the material benefits not enough. Within a year Peter had resigned his post with the RSPB.

At the beginning of May, it was high time to census the breeding birds. Many of the resident species had been setting up territories, making nests and laying eggs since the beginning of April. Some species, like the early nesting mallard ducks and lapwings, already had broods of well-developed chicks.

Repeated walking over the reserve had given me a fair knowledge of its topography. What I lacked was experience of any method which would ensure accuracy over such a varied habitat. The marshes, for instance, with their long concealing vegetation and areas of secluded water, would demand a different approach to the bald machair levels where birds were plain to see.

It seemed that the machair must be the easiest surface on which to count birds and I began with it. For the purpose of censusing, 'machair' was defined as all the sward, cultivated land and sand-dune between the fresh marshes and the sea. It was separable from the headland of Ard an Runair, which, although used for grazing, is rocky and uncultivable, and the damp margins of the marshes and Loch Paible.

I spent a satisfactory day tracing and drawing large-scale maps at a convenient size for use in the field and, armed with half a dozen of these, set out next morning to begin my counts. The correct approach was more obvious than anticipated. On the machair it was necessary, simply, to cover the ground; the same ground, again and again, recording and mapping the birds. If a pair of birds occurred in the same spot, visit after visit, it was reasonably certain that they were nesting there. The precise location of the nests was irrelevant at this stage, as was whether they produced any young. It was necessary merely to know how many pairs of each species attempted to breed.

Winds soft from the sea blew and quietened. Showers followed sunlight and cloud shadows strolled or raced across clean swept levels of turf and marram. Day followed day timelessly as I inched my way over the machair, up and down the edges of cultivated strips where crofters were finishing their sowing; back and forwards meticulously over areas of turf where rabbits and sheep grazed short the sweet grass and daisies.

Birds were identified by their calls, and after repeated visits I recognised individuals and pairs, even anxiously expected them to appear and mob me on their territories. Whatever the weather, I was out from first light to darkness, and at the end of a week had covered scores of maps with little symbols representing birds. A day indoors comparing maps, plotting out individual territories, and a reasonable estimate of the number and variety of birds attempting to breed on the machair could be given.

My skin stung with sunburn, my eyes were strained with hours of intense use of binoculars, but I went on immediately to the marshes. Big mallard chicks were splashing about in the creeks, lapwing chicks were up and running, some birds might even be starting their second nests, and I couldn't afford to take a single day off.

I had dreaded this initial attempt on a systematic count of the birds in the marshes. It seemed such a complex region of interwoven water and land, much of it difficult of access and hidden from sight. And there were so many birds – waders, ducks, grebes, rails, larks, buntings, warblers and pipits – dawn and dusk choruses were deafening and all day the marshes seethed with birds courting, feeding, preening. I sat with a map in Goular cemetery at sunrise of my first day of marsh censusing and felt my first real inadequacy. There was so much going on in the marsh below me, so much inseparable sound and movement of birds, that I didn't know where or how to start.

In the event the process was as inevitable as over the very different machair. The cemetery gave the best possible view over the entire marsh area, but scattered through it were various prominent knolls: old walls, sites of sheepfolds and ruined shielings, usable as points of elevation over marshland immediately around them. By selecting a series of these watching points, I could move from one to another in a censusing 'round', which in its entirety would give close prospects of the whole marsh system.

To minimise disturbance to the birds, I moved from point to point quickly and unobtrusively, and, having achieved each stance, settled and was still enough to allow the birds in my area of vision to behave naturally. By noting the species of birds, their position and behaviour on successive visits, I would eventually be able to say what birds were breeding in that section, which merely calling in to feed, and which passing through on migration. Observations from each section pieced together should finally give a picture of birdlife in the whole marsh.

In the cemetery that morning, twites were flitting around the ancient lichenous memorial to the Clan Ranald Macdonalds, and corn buntings perched singing on the tombstones. North was a prospect over Goular and Hougharry townships to the Haskeir islands, framed by the arms of Hougharry Bay.

Distant views were not for me that morning. Turning away I concentrated attentions on the marshland immediately below. Wildfowl first, since some of them were clearly visible out on the open water. Tufted ducks are late breeders, and there was still a flock of mixed ducks and drakes, out in the middle of the loch. In a very short time they would be less conspicuous, as they paired off and established nesting territories deep in the drier marshes, perhaps hundreds of yards from the nearest open water. This opportunity of counting them before the flock dispersed enabled me to make an early assessment.

The tufted duck is a jaunty black and white diving duck with a crested head, easily recognisable. Other ducks were equally recognisable, given clear views: shovellers with their chestnut flanks and huge spatulate bills; green-headed mallards; teal so much smaller than the other regular species. The only drake which might be difficult was the gadwall; this is a less common species, hard to identify without clear views of their china-white speculae, the even grey vellum of their bodies. Eventually, I identified them by their position in the marsh and mannerisms, but during the initial period they were the most problematical of all the wildfowl.

The trouble with all these dabbling ducks was that they hid themselves away in the shallows, up creeks or under banks of overhanging vegetation, where no matter how bright their colours, they could easily be overlooked. Adding to the problem was the late

Arctic skua chasing an arctic tern

date. Most of the females were sitting on eggs or leading broods of ducklings about in the thick vegetation. The drakes formed post-courting bachelor parties on the loch where they were fairly easy to see, but ducks are notoriously polygamous birds and the number of drakes observed in no way represented the number of nests.

A true picture of wildfowl numbers and distribution became apparent only after prolonged study. Ducklings grew from feathered specks to adult-sized juveniles and I learned just what an incredibly small proportion survives to maturity; finally, and most reward-ingly, how each species of duck uses its habitat and co-exists with other birds of the marsh. By the time that amount of knowledge had been gained the breeding season would be over and these resident birds joined by others of the same and different species, on migration or to spend their winters here. For the present it was possible only to count, identify and translate the activity on the loch into a pattern of coloured crosses on a map.

After dealing with ducks, I moved from the loch to its banks and began to census the waders. There was a problem of separating waders that were nesting from those that had called in on migration, and those that nested elsewhere and had come to the lochside only to bathe, drink and feed. Only after weeks of observation and recording would my maps give an indication of territory size and location for every type of wader breeding on the marsh.

All waders were noted and recorded, but there were a few which could with certainty be dismissed as breeding species. The black-tailed godwits, for instance, were present in the same area for about a week, nine of them, curlew sized but with straight bills like folded scissors, magnificent in their breeding plumage of dark red, white and black. These passage migrants called at the machair marshes on their way to breeding grounds further north. Similarly with the single spotted redshank stalking long-legged at the loch edge, and the ruffs gathered in what seemed perfect lekking stance on a hillock of rabbit-grazed turf. Fascinating birds, these and other regular or vagrant migrants, they were exciting to see and by their presence indicating the richness of the marsh as wader habitat, although they were not really relevant to my present preoccupation with breeding birds.

A basic pattern of wader distribution according to habitat became apparent, even on this first visit. Some species, like snipe and redshanks, were most numerous in and above areas of marshland where cattle and sheep never grazed and the vegetation was most luxuriant. These are the waders which hide their nests in tussocks, or bowered by rushes, sedges and longer grass. Other species, like lapwings and the tiny trilling dunlins, showed a distinct preference for the open, cattle-trodden, softly damp margins of the marshes. Their eggs lie couched in the slightest of depressions, on mere wisps of gathered nest material. These birds which nest in the open are disturbed easily, relying on close camouflage to save their eggs from detection, while the waders which nest in more covered situations sit closely, themselves almost invisible among the tangled shadows of the grass.

By repeatedly associating certain species with a certain sort of terrain, I quickly developed an 'eye' for them. I would squelch across a section of marsh edge and find myself quite prepared for the adult dunlin which suddenly appeared. Walking knee-high among dead umbelliferous plants and sprouting sedges, at some crucial stage I instinctively stepped with more care, all senses keenly alert, and a snipe would dash away from its eggs at my feet.

There was a distinction between the machair and the marsh as wader habitat. Both types of ground are densely populated by waders, but the drier, sandy machair is particularly favoured by species which in other parts of Britain nest along sea-shores, on shingly or sandy beaches. Thus, oystercatchers and ringed plovers nested on the machair, often among the growing corn, where they were later joined by colonies of arctic terns. These machair-breeding species might feed in the marshes and take their young among the long vegetation for protection from predators, but they remained dry habitat nesters, rarely if ever locating their nests in the marsh.

Ringed plover

So, from among all the noise and activity of the most densely packed habitat for waders in Britain, themes, patterns emerged. I learned the necessity for concentration on the work in hand. It was so easy to forget about censusing the birds and lose myself in contemplation: of a single redshank circling and song-flighting; a snipe quivering and ticking clock-like on a fence post; a heron stalking eels up a shallow creek; or to stare in vacant appreciation over marsh and loch to croftlands, moorlands, the distant blue wedge-shape of Eaval.

Sitting in the cemetery, my back propped against the wall of the old Clanranald memorial, I fell into a state of half basking in the May sunshine, half dreamy contemplation of the horizon. A corncrake startled me, the first I had ever heard, but that call was unmistakable, something between a rasp and a rattle, very loud, a stridulating sort of sound like some enormous grasshopper. Not only is the sound loud but it carries, so that on still summer evenings you can hear a corncrake's call miles away across the machair. At close quarters it is simply deafening. The sound came from everywhere; when the second double-crake came, it seemed only inches from my ear.

A skulking bird, so say all the guide-books. Heard more often than seen, rarely taking to flight, this corncrake hopped out of a tussock of dead grass and stood on the drystone wall, erect and defiant of the guide-books, 10yd away at most. Every rust-coloured or golden-brown feather was visible, its big staring eye, its short horny bill. When it called the sound was like some distasteful lump which the bird brought up from its crop. First the head was thrown back, bill open, then body and throat convulsed, neck feathers extended and finally the lump of sound was jerked out. The corncrake looked apopleptic and momentarily nonplussed, then it clicked its head back and called again. It was like some gouty, tweedy old colonel out on a shoot, barking orders at his beaters.

This concrake sat in full view on the wall top for fully ten minutes, and, mindful of the bird's reputation, I watched it intently. This might be exceptional behaviour, I might never again have so clear a view of a corncrake. In fact, for two months that corncrake displayed itself on tombstones and boulders atop the cemetery wall, not only to me but to birdwatchers who were enthralled and to funeral-going groups of crofters who tried to ignore it.

I began to wish that the Goular corncrakes would read the guide-books and behave as they ought, when a pair nested in the nettles behind the RSPB cottage. Until late at night and again at first dawning the creatures would crake incessantly, and on more than one occasion they took shelter from heavy rain under my caravan and craked there, for hours and hours. They are one of Britain's rarest birds and a sought-after speciality of this reserve, but for the sake of sleep and sanity I conditioned myself not to notice them.

106

Corncrake

After the cemetery, the next watching point on my census round was at the tip of a long peninsula which reached far into the middle of Loch nam Feithean and ended in a small dry knoll. Once it had been used by wildfowlers from Balranald House who had heightened the knoll and strengthened it against flood with large stones. In a decade of disuse, grass had grown over this shooters' 'butt' and it now provided me with a natural couch on which to lie or sit. It was a real 'heart of the marsh' situation; on three sides reeds, rushes and open water, and immediately behind a narrow strip of poor flood pasture broken by extensive iris beds. To reach the end of the peninsula involved walking through the territories of innumerable ground-nesting waders. Innumerable, but censusing demanded accurate counting.

Out on the loch there was a variety of ducks, and this was the place from which to watch dabchicks and mute swans, smallest and largest of waterbirds. Several pairs of dabchicks had nest rafts moored into the rushes at the edge of the loch and they were always present, always confiding, swimming and diving nearby and keeping up a constant silvery chatter, the sound of which, of all birdsong, is for me the most expressive of fresh wetland. Hearing it now always brings to mind a Loch nam Feithean bay where bog-bean mats the stems of reed and clubrush, trout surface among floating bistort and water lilies, and dabchicks sport among the flowers.

The mute swans had a nest on the tip of the peninsula, and since it was a traditional site, used for many successive years, the nest had become massive: 3ft deep and 6ft across, a great mat of old and new bog-bean stems and reed, rather like a compost heap on which the pen swan nevertheless looked regal. On my first visit she craned her neck and hissed; as day followed day she became accustomed to me and showed no alarm when I sat within yards of her on the side of the knoll. The cob of this pair spent his days in the middle of the loch, disputing his territory with the cob of another breeding pair, or with a flock of immature birds, some of them possibly his own progeny of previous years. That day, he was busily seeing off a flock of wild whooper swans, driving them away and then in an excess of irritability turning to lunge at a passing teal. He was a constant aggressor until his pen hatched out and fledged five cygnets, when he moderated his behaviour and swam about with his family, benignly paternal, serene.

Another belt of marsh to hurry across, the disturbed noisy waders mobbing and distressing me, brought me to my third watching point. This was a ridge of higher pasture bordering the loch rather like the rim of a saucer. Attempts had been made by the old estate, and more recently by crofters, to drain these pastures, but so far no drainage scheme had succeeded and after every rainy spell the area became a basin glittering with water-flashes of varying depth and size. It was an agriculturalists' nightmare, but snipe and redshanks nested in the rushes, dunlins bred on the damp pasture, and waders and wildfowl of every variety favoured the pools. In winter the entire basin would be under water, an extension of the loch.

I recorded bleating snipe and circling redshanks, plotted pairs of lapwings and dunlins on my map, but all the time was distracted by the gull colony on Loch nam Feithean which in spring dominates this section of the marsh. One hundred and fifty pairs of black-headed gulls and a score of pairs of common gulls were trying to breed on an island 40yd by 10. The island is nowhere more than a foot above the level of the water and it was solid with gulls sitting tail to tail, beak to beak. In this second week of May they were incubating full clutches of eggs, and the gulls wheeling thick as snowflakes above the island were a mixture of off-duty partners and non-breeding birds. Hundreds of them, they mobbed each other and every moving thing that attracted their aggressive fancy.

On some wetland nature reserves, black-headed gulls are considered undesirable predators and their numbers controlled. Often while birdwatching over the marshes, I had been incensed to see the larger gulls attack broods of lapwing chicks and ducklings. The gulls seemed insatiable; they would swallow the chicks whole and alive, one after the other. Often a herring gull sat dyspeptically on a stone, heedless of mobbing waders, gorged to the neck with ducklings and a pair of small feet dangling from its bill. These larger gulls and crows definitely had an effect on the numbers of other birds' young reared from the marshes; but they are a natural control in an area where ground predators are few and I was reluctant to start any campaign of destruction.

Arctic tern

I was particularly reluctant to interfere with the black-headed gull colony since in the weeks since my arrival no predation was evident on chicks by this species. The black-headed gulls are insect and fish eaters, harmless and beautiful followers of ploughs. The colony certainly made the marsh richer, adding its colour and noise to a scene already vital with nesting wildfowl and waders.

It was from this point at the lochside that I saw my first otters at Balranald a week or so later. One beautiful calm morning there was more than the usual agitation among the nesting gulls for two otters were playing along the bank of their island colony. The gulls were hysterical but the otters ignored them, engaged in a catch-me sort of game which went on for a quarter of an hour before it ended in the otters lying side by side on their backs in a bed of bog-bean, clutching with hind- and forepaws at the flowers.

Otter

The rest of my census walk followed higher land, giving good views over a succession of marshy bays, and also into hollows of drier pasture which was bog rather than marsh, and contained several smaller gull colonies as well as the inevitable high density of breeding waders. The ridge ended with a wall, behind which I crouched for my final session, overlooking a wide and very lovely hidden lagoon. I loved that vantage point; there were rabbits and daisies at my feet, and short sweet turf with pansies, trefoil, wild thyme. Skylarks sang over it and although it was part of a wetland habitat, it had clear upland air. I sat there, usually for some time, after finishing my counting; then waded across the wet levels west of Loch nam Feithean back to Goular and the caravan.

At least once a day I walked this census route. Depending on weather and birds, it could take between two and four hours to complete a circuit of the marshes, and after a brief rest at the caravan I would set off for the reed-beds near Balranald House, binoculars around my neck, telescope in its leather case across one shoulder like a rifle, and rucksack on my back containing recording equipment, flasks and a great deal of food. I was perpetually hungry those days, and when setting out from the caravan, never knew precisely when I would be back. There seemed a great deal to do, a lot of reserve to cover. The marshes demanded the slowest, most detailed examination, but daily trips to the Paible marshes and Ard an Runair were necessary and all the western beaches. Hating to think that anything within the 1,500 acres of the reserve would escape my attention, I was always mobile, restless, vigilant.

To reach the reed-beds I crossed the machair, keeping an eye out for flocks of golden plovers, which could look like cow-pats patterning the grass or stubble on fallow stretches, or for any late geese which might have come in during the night. Sometimes my route was varied to meet some working crofter on his strip of ploughed land. I tried to make these meetings seem casual, just passing by. Out in the field and engaged so exclusively on bird work, I was afraid of losing contact with local people and seeming to them only a distant figure involved in affairs quite other than theirs. Some 'casual' meetings on the machair were pleasant and a means of maintaining slight contact until more time could be given to the public relations side of my job.

I patrolled the perimeter of the reed-beds, jumping iris-chocked drainage ditches and struggling with wire fences in all stages of disrepair. Still days were welcome, since the main birds of the reeds were small songsters, recorded by hearing rather than sight. Sedge warblers were particularly difficult to spot, slim reed-coloured birds which stay down among the stems in rough weather. Given a calm day and warm sunshine, however, they cling swayingly to the extreme tips of the reeds and sing as if making up for lost opportunity. The song is a tuneless scratchy chattering, but half a dozen or so gave the dead reed stems an appropriate voice. After so much con-

Reed bunting

centration on waders and wildfowl, the sedge warblers were as welcome as nightingales.

The reeds also held a few pairs of reed buntings, dumpy little birds with a faint, melancholy song. In sunshine the male buntings would cease to be dull brown birds as their plumage showed chestnut and russet, their black heads finely moustached with yellow and white. Then they were almost as eyecatching as the red-chested male stonechats which held territory along the overgrown remains of a wall which ran alongside the reeds.

There was no real reason to push into the heart of the marsh, but I liked to sit concealed, listening to the warblers and the whispering of the reeds. Stillness and concealment occasionally had its reward when a hen harrier or short-eared owl came wafting over, not seeing me until directly overhead. The harriers swung away immediately, but the owls were more curious and sometimes hovered a few feet above me, glaring down with surprised marigold eyes.

Because of the many waders which nested there, Loch Paible basin was at least as deserving of study as the fresh-marshes of Loch nam Feithean. By contrast, only a few corn buntings and skylarks nested in the crests of the sand-dunes. On the lower, more gently sloping backs of the dunes were ringed plover nests among daisies and yellow pansies. Their sand-coloured eggs were incredibly hard to find, the birds themselves difficult enough to spot as they sat low on the nests or stood among the thickening carpet of flowers. I never tried very hard to find the nests, content to locate and record the paired birds, and watch them run jerkily to and fro at my feet.

The plovers had soft, throbbing calls, totally unlike the oyster-catchers which shared this habitat. Oystercatchers were so headachingly, shrilly insistent, that they of all the mobbing waders could make me look forward to peaceful days at the end of the birds' breeding season.

The dunes levelled out to a plain of machair sward, and here on strips of ploughed and fallow land ringed plovers and oystercatchers were fewer, supplanted by lapwings. Lapwings and machair ploughland invariably went together, but here above Paible the strips of fallow stubble also supported a colony of thirty arctic terns. The sharp white wings of the terns and scissoring swallow-like forked tails glanced among the slow broad-winged lapwings. Plaintive plover calls and the terns' raucous screaming: here, as in the marshes, my recording was inhibited by the abundance and diversity of the birds, an almost irresistible tendency to stop the recording and busy pencil, and sit or stand and simply marvel.

Below the ploughland was a zone of habitat which fell enigmatically between damp pasture and salt-marsh. Flooded by exceptionally high, wind-driven tides some winters, it was dissected like the salt-marsh, yet the vegetation was as long and tangled as that in a freshwater bog. It held an unusually high density of nesting redshanks and dunlin, waders whose respective preference for long or short vegetation separated them over the rest of the reserve.

Finally, fringing the estuarine sands and muds was a crescent of salt-marsh. To some extent flooded by every high tide, it held no nesting birds but was important in the ornithological picture since it gave nesting wildfowl and waders from a wide area places to shelter, roost and feed, and its deep narrow creeks provided cover for small chicks of all species. Early in the season the salt-marshes were empty except for a few shelducks which nested in rabbit holes in nearby dunes. By June the marshes looked like a nursery, broods of ducklings and waders everywhere among its creeks and brackish pools. The salt-marshes were perpetually fascinating, a terrain intermediate between inlet and pasture; open and airy as a sand-flat, yet intimate as the unploughed corner of a field.

Thrilled immediately by Loch nam Feithean marshes, after a while I fell quietly in love with Loch Paible. More than the spectacularly abundant marshes, it expressed the genus loci of the west Uist coast. At ebb-tide in the afternoons, I sat by the ruin of a shieling above the salt-marshes, looking over machair and estuary to the crofts of Paible township scattered along the opposite shore. It was a wild scene, but emphatically human. A crofter drove his line of cattle slowly from the machair through the salt-marshes and out

A typical Uist saltmarsh near Claddach Kirkibost, grazed by crofters' sheep into a flat lawn

over estuarine sands towards the township. Birds mobbed the procession and curlews on the sand-flats flew away, wailing. There seemed precious little distinction between ploughed land, estuarine levels and incult moorland, and little to separate man and beast and bird.

Every day, after examining the birds above Loch Paible, if the tide allowed, I walked out across the sands and muds of the inlet to the central channel, and followed it to the sea. Many migrants were using the sands: greenshanks, grey plovers, parties of knots rosy in summer plumage. Waders of the same species favoured the same patch of inlet at every low tide. Ringed plovers regularly flocked to the harder sands at the head, while the longer-billed dunlins preferred the softer muds beside tributary creeks. Curlews and redshanks stalked about in the salt-marsh and turnstones indefatigably rummaged in areas where seaweeds collected. Greenshanks liked the sea pools; oystercatchers gathered at the rocky inlet mouth where they could feed on limpets, mussels and winkles.

I derived constant pleasure from the regular birds, but could still

thrill to the vagrant, the rarity. One evening I had just walked past a
shallow sand pool when a soft but penetrating call made me turn
back. Five little stints had come in unseen; smallest of European
waders, intricately patterned in black and brown, standing in a row
at the edge of the pool. Next day they had gone, no doubt on
another leg on their journey to breeding grounds in the Arctic.

Another uncommon species which particularly appealed was the
long-tailed duck, a small sea duck which winters around Scottish
coasts but breeds further north. The ducks which collected at the
mouth of Loch Paible in May were in full mating fervour, and they
splashed about the skerries playfully, making calls which were
crooning, tender, more like voices of flocking doves than wildfowl.

After Paible, it was a long trek up the western beaches birdwatching all the way to Ard an Runair and a change of terrain. The rocky
headland was notable for its colonies of arctic terns which arrived
during the first week of May, and for the exceptionally high
densities of ringed plovers and oystercatchers, both nesting on
short, salt resistant swards behind the rocky shore. This was attractive habitat, strewn with seashells, starred with daisies, and made a
marine garden by cushions of flowering sea-pinks.

I tried to calculate the number of terns in their colonies without
disturbing them too much. Self protection encouraged caution, as
the terns were extremely aggressive, likely to attack, peck and draw
blood from scalp or defensively upflung forearms and hands. It was
prudent to watch from a respectful distance and admire their fishing
skills in the sea off the headland, the swallowlike grace and

Arctic terns

Little tern

buoyancy of their flighting between colony and sea, and their ethereal transparency when upflung against intense sunlight.

Near the arctic terns, but in a separate colony, nested three pairs of little terns, and they were more fetching. Once widespread around the coast of Britain, these smallest of our terns are now quite rare, having suffered from increased human pressure on the beaches where they nest. The Outer Hebrides have many miles of virtually unvisited shellsand strand and it may be that the islands are now the little terns' stronghold in Britain. Rarity and vulnerability added to their charm and they were special among the reserve's birds. They seemed creatures of sky and light more than land, their movements so sharp, erratic, their shape attenuated and voices high-pitched to near inaudibility, a thin wire-like shrieking. They laid their eggs on the headland but their link with greensward was tenuous and brief. After a week or two all the nests failed for some reason and by June the little terns had gone.

The headland was the best place on the reserve for seabirds, both those breeding locally like the gannets, black guillemots and fulmar petrels, and passing migrants like the skuas and chains of shearwaters which trailed by in hundreds, rising and dipping close to the waves. It may have been a reaction against the preponderance of large, noisy, oceanic birds which made me select as special favourites the twites, little finches of the machair, half a dozen pairs of which nested among the headland's rocks and tussocks of heather. Their neat, grass-lined nests contained pale blue spotted eggs, and they reminded me of hedgerow nests in more familiar habitat. While the gannets plunged offshore and the skuas harried the screaming terns, I sat among the rocks studying the sparrow-like twites, hoping they would give me, among all that raucous wildness, a short burst of melodious song.

So my days were spent, most of May. Long, happy, tiring days of sunshine and showers, walking and sitting, watching and recording. My daily round took eight or ten hours to complete, and after a late supper in the caravan, I wrote the day's notes into a log book and work diary. Sometimes sunsets would flare across the west-facing windows. The Tilley lamp hissed while corncrakes grated and moorhens cackled outside in the dark. Always while writing I fought against sleep, a desperate battle to keep eyes open until the last bird was recorded, the last comment made. Then in a dreamlike drowsiness I'd unroll the sleeping-bag and stretch out on the caravan seat. All the waterbirds and waders, rails and gulls and sea-birds vocal in Balranald's night-time marshes couldn't prevent me from falling instantly asleep.

Guillemot

Gannets

Active as were those days, I still longed for some closer relationship with the reserve. A crofter could work all day, earning a living
from the land, and his claim to proprietorship would be as valid as
mine. Other Balranald wardens must have spent their spring season
similarly. I sought some special experience which would make the
area uniquely mine, justify my possessive love for it.

So on fine nights I dragged myself out again, to sleep in the open.
If less than exhausted by the day, I'd set out at dusk, but more often
woke by alarm clock at 3am, hiked out by starlight or moonlight to
my chosen spot and lay there half sleeping, half awake, while the
sky paled and morning came to the island. Sleep claimed me once
the sun was warm on my face, the magic of dawn finished.

Nights like this on the marshes were too noisy for sleep. All night
those marshes boiled and crackled, but I could have dozed through

identifiable sound, even the snipe thrumming yards from my head and corncrakes stumbling into the sleeping-bag and braying their surprise into my ear. Preventing sleep were other noises. There are no hippopotami in Uist and crofters weren't given to midnight bathing, but splashes too loud for duck or crofter would happen and I'd have to get up and investigate, always to stare bewildered at water still or gently ruffled, undisturbed in the moonlight. Nothing there, but my mind would create fantasies and there'd be no sleep for the remainder of that night.

Most peaceful and memorable nights out during that period were those by Loch Paible, a favoured spot, and as dawn arrived I lay with my head propped back, looking with the light as it spread and strengthened over the estuarine sands. There were many birds and once a curious otter sniffed at my rucksack; but the companions remembered most of those Paible nights were the curlews. They shifted with the tide, but generally during low-tide mornings they would flight in at dawn from their roosts on shore rocks, in fresh-marsh and salt-marsh, and take their first food of the day on the sands. They came in ones and twos and dozens until there were hundreds of curlews, clustering in the soft-edged creeks and probing out over the level surface among strands of seaweeds and wormcasts. Their flighting shapes showed dimly against sky before sunrise, then their angularity became defined as daylight strengthened and they stalked about, actively feeding.

They called as they came in, and crooned to each other as they fed, and at some indeterminate hour they called again, the sound building in strength and intensity until they left; in singles and small parties. By full daylight, when the sun was strong and the smell of warmed tideline seaweed noticeable, the inlet was empty of curlews. Only the small wading birds with their smaller voices remained, laying claim to the sands.

Such days and nights cost me sleep and human companionship, but they sharpened my awareness of the reserve. As time passed, I seemed to develop a foreknowledge of what birds would be found in any particular place, given certain conditions of time, tide and weather. On occasion, I deviated from route and routine without wholly knowing why; impelled to some spot, I would find an unusual bird or witness some exceptionally interesting incident. My experience during the censusing period was a mixture of fact and impression, creature and scene, and it gave me more than a factual cognisance of numbers and species. At the end of six extraordinarily intense weeks the reserve was incontestably 'mine'.

Although Balranald's main claim to natural history fame must be its spectacular densities of breeding waders, it is also important as a stop-off point for birds on migration. The habitat is extremely suitable for attracting a variety of birds; beaches and estuarine inlet for waders, coastal fresh-marshes for wildfowl, sand-dunes and shoreline crannies for anything requiring shelter and rest.

The whooper swans which had entertained me at the caravan window were the first of the winter birds to leave. I saw them go, head-on into a storm cloud, one morning in early April. Then the other wildfowl became restless, and the habitual flock of greylag geese disappeared from the marsh, probably on a very short migration to nesting places on North Uist's inland moors. The wigeon flock vanished, other duck species diminished in number, leaving only the summer residents to mix with migrants which stayed only a day or two before moving on. A rare American wigeon stayed for three days; a pair of pintail came and looked hieratic among mallard and gadwall. I hoped the pintails would stay and breed, but they graced the marshes for only a week.

It was fascinating, this spring movement of birds. But no feature of the season was more stirring than the mass migrations of geese, those long trailing Vs of birds wavering up from the south, passing over and heading northwards, following the islands towards Iceland and Greenland.

Even the stoical crofters were affected. Many times they would stop me on my rounds to mention parties of this or that species they had noticed. During April and early May, geese were as constant a topic of conversation as weather and tides. I was humbled by their superior ability to identify the different goose species. Iain from The Glebe was particularly expert, and it was he who first taught me the difference between the calls of greylags, whitefronts and pinkfeet, and how to identify them by darker or lighter plumages, nuantic differences in size, proportion, and mannerisms of flight.

Old Cameron could hardly be expected to be moved by geese or any natural phenomenon, but one day he surprised me. It was a sunny calm morning and I was taking an hour off to do some very necessary clothes washing. Marching my bundle of clothes to the tap, I passed Cameron who for once was outdoors, repairing his fence and gate. He took his work casually. He was sitting cross-legged over a post hole, spooning gently at the sandy soil with a short-handled dustpan. Jacketless in the warm sun, he wore his shirt open at the neck and on his feet, carpet slippers. I stopped briefly to agree what a lovely morning and passed on. I took possession of the wooden tub from drinking bullocks and was wetting my first batch of clothes when Cameron dropped his dustpan with a clang and came running up the track, slippers absurdly flapping. There must be some health or domestic crisis; but no, it was geese.

'Those geeses, they wee plack puggers off the Monachs, they've come to the Ard.' He pointed to Ard an Runair, the crest of headland and standing stone visible over the dunes of Hougharry Bay. At first I saw nothing, but Cameron was insistent.

'Look,' he said, clutching my arm. 'Listen. You can hear them, plain as anything.' It was like the barking of a very distant pack of dogs, scarcely audible, above the sighing of the sea. I stared hard and at last saw a movement, just discernible, as if the horizon itself flexed and shifted. It was a huge pack of geese, walking just over the skyline. A party of twenty or so took flight, circled, and dropped back into the general movement. The goose pack kept walking, towards the summit of the headland, now coming into plainer view, dark and cohesive as a cloud shadow, but moving against the wind. I thanked Cameron, raced with my unwashed clothes to the caravan and flung them sodden into a corner, grabbed binoculars and notebook, and ran for the headland.

There were about two and a half thousand geese, probably the

Barnacle geese

entire flock of barnacle geese which winters on the Monach or Heiskeir Islands, west of North Uist. They are beautiful birds, black and grey, white faced, considerably smaller than the usual grey geese, and smaller billed for grazing the swards of salt-marsh, tundra or machair. They seemed essentially northern, creatures of glacier and waste, the least 'domestic' of all our wild geese.

They were heading for nest sites in Greenland, but for the moment they seemed part of the wintry headland, the bleached pasture, bare rocks, the sheets of floodwater in every hollow. The whole enormous flock kept tightly together, like some army on the move, and walked, grazing as they went, across the top of the headland and down its slopes to the shore. There, above the rocks, the army consolidated and waited.

They were still there in the evening, in the same place. It was as if they were expecting some sign from the north as summons; perhaps they were and it came during the night, since in the morning they were gone. Had it not been for Cameron's acute, almost extra-sensory perception of the geese, I would have done my washing and possibly missed the flock. But Cameron had witnessed the migratory gathering of Heiskeir barnacles to Ard an Runair every spring and autumn for more than seventy years.

Migration affected routines more seriously in early June, when one misty morning a disorientated gannet crash-landed in a crofter's garden near Bayhead. The crofter was an elderly widow, one of The Glebe Macdonalds' ubiquitous relatives, and she telephoned Mary who relayed the news to me via Iain on his cattle-tending rounds. By the time this tortuous grapevining had done its work, the gannet had been in the care of the crofting lady for two days.

Her house was one of the few traditionally shaped and reed-thatched cottages remaining on Uist. A fresh-complexioned woman met me at the door, wearing a woollen beret, clean striped apron and wellington boots. She invited me in, and the kitchen, though earth floored and dark, had a homely peat-smokey smell and looked clean. The kettle came off its stand by the stove and a cup of tea was inside me before the gannet was mentioned.

It wass a kind of big white duck, she wass thinking, or maybe it would be a goose. The poor thing. It wass after hurting itself and it couldn't fly at all, so it was in a bucket in the byre. A bit cramped, but it was doing very well; she had been feeding it on cabbage and porridge. Indeed it wass company, the creature, but perhaps I'd better have it, because being the bird man and all, I'd know how to put it right.

A cabbage-eating gannet in a bucket defied credulity, but I followed her out to the byre. It was a gannet, and it was in an empty oil-drum, not a bucket. It was also in a vile temper, weaving its 6in dagger of a bill towards us over the rim of the drum and glaring with its mad seabird's blue eye. How had she got it in there, and how, for goodness sake, did she feed it? It was easy to lift the bird, she explained, once she had thrown a blanket over it. As for the feeding, that wasn't so simple. Ruefully she showed me the backs of her hands which had been severely, deeply gashed. The raking cuts ran up her wrists to her forearms.

She showed me how she managed the feeding. A saucepan by the oil-drum was filled with a mash of oatmeal and cabbage, and, scooping out a handful, she held it out towards the bird. The gannet lunged murderously, beak wide for a two-pronged stab, and as it lunged the woman threw in her handful of porridge. Some may indeed have gone down its gullet, certainly the gannet clapped its beak shut and swallowed hard. It was obvious how the woman had collected those gashes, and I marvelled at her persistence, her spontaneous pity for the injured creature.

Using the blanket, we bundled the gannet into my van and it was driven to Goular and placed in an empty wooden chest in the cottage. Wardens do not normally accept the care of injured birds. It is a time-consuming, useless business as the birds rarely survive, and if they do, are even less frequently fully rehabilitated. In some special cases a warden might pass on an injured bird to a vet or the RSPCA, but gannets are not a threatened species; like all birds their deaths are naturally violent and legions of them perish annually of exposure or starvation.

Nevertheless, this crofting lady had taken a great deal of trouble with her gannet and would certainly ask about its welfare via her relatives at The Glebe. There was no one nearby to whom it could be passed for more expert treatment, so against all reason and inclination, I tried to keep it alive.

A pair of visiting birdwatchers was coerced into helping me examine the gannet. We could find nothing amiss with it, except emaciation, probably a result of its

Gannet

recent porridge diet. If it could be fed, it might recover. This proved more problematical than anticipated. Gannets eat fish and on this island of fishermen-crofters, fresh fish are simply not to be had. In August maybe, if a herring boat came loaded to Lochmaddy, a full cran might be bought for next to nothing; or if the weather was warmer, trout caught in the lochs. Meanwhile, what few local fishermen there were, fished exclusively for lobsters, and the trout were lying low, uncatchable. Why not do what every housewife on the island does, and buy frozen fish fingers from Bayhead shop?

I bought the fish fingers and Patricia came twice a day to help force-feed the gannet. It spat them out and visibly weakened. Corned beef was cut into fish-slim strips and dipped in sea-water; the gannet regurgitated them in pools of green, evil-smelling bile. It resisted all our misplaced attentions and I was relieved when, after a week, it died. I carried it by the legs to Hougharry Bay and threw it as far as possible into the ebbing tide, resolving never again to take charge of an ailing bird, especially a seabird. Let them die peacefully in the ocean, where they belong.

Censusing had made it necessary to concentrate not only on wildlife, but also on the reserve area. For six weeks or so I had hardly left Balranald, and so when this period was over felt a natural urge to explore. North Uist was still largely unknown to me; there were other places of extreme interest and I was determined not to become one of those wardens exclusively obsessed by their 'patch'.

When Iain asked me to help him with a day's peat-cutting on the moors it seemed just the right sort of break to take from the reserve. A pleasant and productive change, to do some hard manual work, see something of the interior moorlands and be in the company of local people. Peat-cutting is a conspicuous business and it would do no harm for the people of the township to see me working with one of themselves, at one of their regular tasks.

Most of the peat-cutting is done in April and May, during the first spell of dry weather. The banks are opened and it takes two people no more than three or four days to cut enough peats for the coming year. Cutting need not therefore conflict too much with the other tasks of spring, ploughing, sowing, early lambing; but the actual cutting of the peat is only the start of a lengthy business.

When the peats are cut from the bog they are spread out flat on the heather beside the bank. It takes several consecutive days of rainless weather to dry the upper surfaces of the slabs of peat, then they are propped up in small groups, like sheaves of corn, for the winds to dry them completely. After a week or two, the small stacks are gathered into larger ones. Lastly, they are brought in from the moor and carefully built into the rain-resistant peat-stacks which

Lifting potatoes at Hastin

stand by every island croft-house. Spells of fine weather are necessary to all the stages of peat harvesting, and in a good year a crofter might have his new peat-stack at the door by July, before the corn harvest. In a bad year, the townships may be salvaging what they can of their sodden peats between work on late corn harvests and potatoes, a last miserable rush to gather something in before November gales and darkness make all forms of outdoor work difficult.

The Macdonalds had already cut and gathered their main supply into small stacks. They were ahead with their work and Murdo decided that Iain could afford the time to open and cut an additional small bank, an extra supply to be held in reserve against a longer or colder winter than usual. There could never be too many peats at your door; if you didn't need them yourself they were there to give away. It was unthinkable that anyone should be without a lifegiving peat fire.

It was 10 o'clock of a bright summery morning before we made a move to the peat banks. Crofters rarely start early on their major tasks, there are so many little jobs to be done about the house and byre. Murdo was making a coffin, it was Mary's day for helping with dinners at the school and Iain had to milk the cow and collect the eggs from two dozen hens. A cup of tea, Murdo's brother called in for a chat and to borrow the trailer; but no one hurried, showed impatience. The weather was fine and in June the island days are long.

At last we piled tools, dogs, ourselves, a kettle and food for the day into Iain's pick-up, and drove off down the west coast of the island. The peat bank was with the rest of Hougharry township's cuttings, close to the main road. At one time each crofting family had its peat bank in moorland near the house. Peats were brought back in horse-carried panniers. Now there were no horses, the peat banks were reachable by tractor from a road, and the crofters rented their banks in township units from the estate which owns most of the moors.

Iain's bank ran at right angles to the road, near a large freshwater loch. It was a good place to be working on such a day, the loch surface was wind ruffled, the flat moorlands gave a feeling of space and freedom, yet they were friendly enough when warmed by sun.

The first job was to chop a layer of moss and heather off the top of the bank. Iain flung off his jacket and began work at a great pace, delving out huge cubes of solid saturated moor and heaving them far into the hollow of the bank. I was impressed by his strength, the thrusting power of his wiry arms; but bursts of prodigious energy, showing immense muscular power, are the islanders' speciality. They are trained to this sporadic rather than rhythmical way of working, by much handling of animals and machinery, controlling the sudden movements of sheep and cattle and dealing brusquely with boats and tractors. Iain's strength exceeded mine by far, but he worked in bursts, with many stops. I matched him in stamina and kept pace by working in my own steadier rhythm.

Like this we worked until 1 o'clock, when all the top layer of turf was stripped off and the peat below was a gleaming black shelf, smooth and ready for slicing. We tidied the chunks of thrown-off turfs into a smooth surface on the floor of the bank, a conservationary measure insisted on by the estate. One future day those turfs might be the surface of another layer of peat-cutting.

Iain went to the loch with the kettle, and I lit a fire in the peat bank, using sprigs of heather, with dry pieces of peat and a fire-lighter brought from The Glebe. We shared Iain's tea. It was as black as peat water, it tasted of burnt heather, and when Iain added a fistful of sugar and milk from a tin, the drink was made into food. Our lunch provided by Mary was an equally sustaining combination of the traditional and contemporary. Hard-boiled eggs, home-baked oatcakes and scones, a pot of Mary's own delicious crowdie, with sandwiches of shop-bought bread and jam, a handful of tinsel-wrapped chocolate biscuits and two bananas. Old and new, it satisfied our work-sharpened hungers.

Resting after his food, Iain became talkative. Never unduly withdrawn, he was nevertheless the taciturn type, and it took work and a full belly to loosen his tongue. I said something about the recreational nature of work on the moor in fine June weather. People in cities would pay to be allowed to do it, but it was part of the lucky crofters' regular routine. Iain took me seriously. He didn't want to be a crofter all his days, he confided. He hadn't chosen the job, had he? Then why, simply because of the place and circumstance of his birth, should he necessarily spend all his life farming The Glebe?

What did he really want to do? I asked. He didn't know. Perhaps in the end he might decide to be a crofter. What he asked was a wider experience of occupation and place, and the opportunity to make an eventual choice. 'It's too much to ask,' I said. 'Most people don't have the opportunity to live as you do. Take my advice and choose now to carry on as you are, because experience will only take away any chance you have of being content.'

Iain was silent, sceptical. He looked across his island moors, quivering now with heat haze. When he was younger, still at

Curlew

school, he said, he had fully intended to go to sea, join the Merchant Navy. 'But my father wouldn't let me, being the eldest and all, I'd have to stay and take on the croft.' Iain was silent again, briefly. Then he burst out: 'And now, would you believe it, he won't even let me have a wee fishing boat out in the bay.' The most treacherous offshore waters in Europe and a father's possessive love for his firstborn. I made no comment.

'Do you still think of going to sea?' Iain smiled at that: no, no, he had got over that ambition, it was the foolish whim of a schoolboy. In fact, he'd settled down resignedly, until the wardens started coming to the new bird reserve. They had made him restless again; they were young but they had seen so much, had different jobs in different places.

Now me, with my softer hands than Iain, my lesser strength. Not so very much older than he, but I had lived in different parts of England, Wales, the Highlands. Iain had never been further than Skye, had spent only one night away from The Glebe, at a clay pigeon shoot in Portree. What right had I to talk about the superior value of roots, family, community, a small self-sufficient territory in which to live and work one's days? I was free of the restrictions of family, or church, or the croft, and could wander about exploring, free as one of the birds that were my career.

A hawk-shaped bird with long pointed wings came slanting over the moor. It skimmed the loch, indistinct against sparkling water, then it leaped upwards and was lost against the bright ball of the sun.

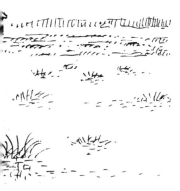

'A skua,' I said, after a moment.
'Aye,' said Iain.
We couldn't think of anything else to say to each other just then, and threw ourselves with unnecessary vigour back to work.

For skinning the turves from the top of the bank we had used ordinary flat-bladed field spades. Now, in cutting the peats themselves, Iain used the traditional tuskeir, a tool adapted specially for peat-cutting. The different peat-cutting regions have their own variations in tools and in methods of work. In Lewis, for instance, the women cut peats while the men stay at home, weaving; in Shetland it is a one-man job. In Uist it is exclusively the males who do the cutting and they always work in pairs, one prising the peats away from the bank, the other throwing them up out of the bank to lie in rows drying on the heather.

The North Uist tuskeir is about 4ft long, the handle straight with the blade. The blade is a right angle of sharpened iron which is pushed vertically into the peat, the user pressing with one foot on a narrow trap. The cutter stands on the surface of the shelf of peat, the thrower stands in the bank, taking each slab off the spade as it is thrust downwards. In good peat no levering is necessary. It is the consistency of soft cheese and falls easily away from the blade. Inferior quality peat is fibrous, brown rather than black, and cutting is more strenuous. Levering each peat free from the bank disturbs the regular rhythm of the work.

Traditionally, the bank is five peats wide, three peats deep, and it requires a certain amount of skill to cut peats of the even size necessary to convenient stacking when dried. Stones might intrude into the bank or the surface texture vary, collapsing into mossy hollows. The cutter varies his stroke according to the depth and width of the shelf on which he stands.

Throwing out the peats demands judgement to achieve rows with no peats overlapping, but the main requirement is brute strength. Each peat is a wedge of solid moor, 6in by 3 at the top and 18in long. Water presses out of them and the weight is formidable, especially when they are thrown from the third layer down.

Iain did the cutting, I the throwing. He pushed the tuskeir in and I took the toppling peat, threw it, and swung back from my throw to another peat toppling for me to take. I liked the feel of the peat, not sticky or black on the hands, but cleanly wet and lukewarm. Each peat thrown out had my handprint on it and holes where my gripping thumbs had sunk in. The Macdonalds might burn these peats, but they carried my mark, they were mine.

Wind came in ripples over the face of the moor, shook heather on the top of the bank and carried on as ruffles across the loch. A good drying wind for the peats, and warmth in the sun, although it was now in the western sky, throwing the floor of the peat bank into

Golden eagle

shadow. We cut the top two layers almost without stopping, had a break for more tea and scones, and when we returned to cut the last layer by mutual assent I took the tuskeir and Iain did the throwing.

A couple of amusing mis-shapes. 'We'll put those on one side for you,' said Iain, throwing them far out across the moor; then I had the feel of the tuskeir and the peat, the rhythm came connecting the moor to me to Iain, and the peats slapped one after the other out onto the heather.

We finished the job, and there was still light in the sky. I felt satisfied but not tired, as if while the sun was still high there was something more to be done to bring the day perfectly to a close. Iain felt the same.

'Are you interested in eagles? I could show you a nest not a far walk from here.' This surprised me on two counts. That Iain should be interested enough to have searched out an eyrie, and that eagles should nest in such flat moorland country. I expected them to be confined to the more mountainous, uninhabited regions of the island's east coast.

This was more buzzard country. Iain may have made the common mistake of confusing the two species, but even so, a buzzard's nest would be a welcome change from all those waders on the machair. Eagles do indeed nest on the Uist moors quite close to human settlement, and most crofters know the locations of the traditional sites. Many are antagonistic to eagles, accusing them of attacking live healthy lambs and even fully grown sheep. A few are sympathetic towards and even proud of their eagles, willing to show them off to interested tourists. Iain's interest had been encouraged by his contact with the Balranald wardens, and since The Glebe sheep were not threatened by a nearby territory, he was a defender rather than a persecutor of the birds.

We walked from the peat bank, Iain setting off at a great pace. His long powerful legs brushed through rank heather as if it wasn't there and he strode uphill faster then I could run down. I followed, too breathless and too tactful anyway to voice doubts about the identity of his birds.

On a low watershed behind the peat banks, golden plovers flew close to us and called. They had nests with eggs or young, but there is no anxiety or indignation in a plover's unvarying single-noted cry. It is like the wind among stones, melancholy. Nothing is more expressive of the desolation of wide uninhabited moorland, unless it is the call of a red-throated diver on some lochan; and we could hear those too, with the plovers making a duet of utter misery.

Over the watershed we were out of sight of the road in a world of watery moorland and birds. It could have been some scene from the arctic fringe of Siberia, never the Britain of cider orchards and hedgerows. Iain led round the flank of a hill, and we came to the edge of a wide shallow valley, quite unsuspected from below.

'There,' said Iain, pointing. Over the hilltop hung an eagle, no mistaking those great vulture-like wings, primaries uptilted and widely splayed. It was stationary in the sky some distance away, but it dominated the whole valley. This was the male bird, the female presumably sitting on a nest somewhere nearby. It puzzled me that there were no cliffs in the valley, not even an outcrop to give site for an eyrie. I couldn't doubt Iain now, however, and stumbled on unquestioningly in his wake through the heather. At a low ridge he stopped and pulled me close to him.

'Stick your head over the ridge and see if she's there.' Thirty yards away a flat-topped rock was embedded in the hillside. On the top of the rock was a large flattish heap of dead heather and other moorland vegetation, and on the top of the heap with her head turned away from me sat the hen eagle.

Iain crawled up beside me. 'She's there then,' he said in an unemphatic but satisfied voice, not much louder than a whisper, but the eagle must have heard him. She swung her massive beak round and glared directly at us with her deep-set golden-brown eyes; no escaping that stare and as she saw us she threw herself off the nest.

There was a moment of fear as she seemed to come straight towards us, huge wings outspread. Eagles rarely attack human intruders; in fact, song-thrushes and tawny owls are much more aggressive at the nest and there are far more records of wounds inflicted by terns and harriers. I just saw a 7ft wing-span fill the sky, had a glimpse of beak and yellow, clenched talons, and instinctively shrank into the heather. She came within inches of us, gathering momentum and uplift to escape; then, with a sound like a gale in trees, she threshed twice, over the hill in a glide and out of sight.

At the nest we examined one pathetic, puling chick, a couple of dismembered grouse and the wing of a mallard. To deliberately disturb an eagle from its nest like this is strictly illegal. As a warden, I was equipped with licenses authorising me to examine the nests of eagles and other rare birds as part of my job, yet was conscious of the enormity of the incident. All that weight and power of an adult eagle displaced, and this scrawny but precious mite of a chick exposed to any passing gull or crow.

We left quickly and, back at the watershed, flopped down again to hide in the heather and looked back. The male eagle was the first to reappear, turning in a slow spiral as if unconcerned above the hilltop. Twenty minutes later the hen came in a fast, compressed glide over the shoulder of the hill, heading directly for the nest. Fortunately she had returned before any harm befell the chick.

We lingered for a while on the watershed, as the moorland darkened around us and the golden plovers made their sad piping. I felt the fascination of the moors, the big inhospitable landscape with its few but specialised and fugitive birds and other animals, and no people. Such a contrasting attraction to the machair teeming with life and colour, but equally strong, even more characteristic of the island. The machair was only a narrow strip up the west coast; most of North Uist was solemn watery moorland just like this.

Iain was silent, no doubt equally affected by the fullness of the day, now the reflective evening. Tomorrow he would be engaged on his croft-work; tomorrow and for years. For a moment I envied him his permanent place on the island, but didn't tell him so, and we drove in our comfortable silence back to The Glebe, where Mary first chid us for being late, then fed us like prodigals returned.

As it happened, my visit to the eagles' nest with Iain was timely, as I was shortly given full opportunity to indulge a new enthusiasm for the moors. A few days later, a request came from the RSPB for me to examine the eagle situation in Uist, find all occupied eyries, and report on the eventual success or failure of each nest. There was concern about the status of the golden eagle in Scotland and the society wanted information about the degree of persecution by crofters and egg collectors.

It was a task accepted gladly. It had touched me, the impressive size of those adult eagles, and the paradoxical vulnerability of the chick in its too easily approachable nest. My protective instinct was roused; also, while looking at eagles I would learn more about the topography and other distinctive wildlife of the moors.

Iain was too occupied to come with me on my inland expeditions, but I didn't always have to walk the moors alone as Patricia often welcomed a break from her house renovations and gardening. Together we approached the huge complex of raised bog and mire, freshwater loch and sea inlet, that comprises the centre of North Uist. Working from the Lochmaddy road northwards, for the sake of maintaining direction we followed the shore of Loch Scadavay, the largest single stretch of freshwater in the island.

A dozen miles in length, at its widest a mile or so across, Scadavay itself has many large and small islands, and a few of these islands have their own tiny lochs. The shoreline of the main loch is indented into innumerable bays and peninsulas, and to follow the shore all the way round the loch would take several days of the most arduous bogtrotting. We had to skirt the largest bays, and cut across the necks of peninsulas, trying to select the most interesting places for exploration.

It was all very much in contrast to my previous hill- or moorland-walking experience. When hill-walking, you follow ridges which gain height easily and avoid the wettest hollows and longest vegetation. But then the objectives are different – long distances covered, free walking and comprehensive views. Searching for wildlife, Patricia and I deliberately selected the lowest lying, wettest stretches of bogland. We flogged across dreary levels of peat hags, and we kept dropping back to Loch Scadavay to stare through binoculars at its islands and open waters.

A hill-walker adopts a rhythmical, ground-devouring stride and keeps going. We ploughed slowly across the surface of a vast saturated sponge. We heaved our feet out of sucking sphagnum, threaded tortuously through tussocky sedge and deer grass, battled with waist-high heather and clambered agonisingly in and out of steep-sided soft-bottomed peat hags. We stopped often, to consult the map, to examine more closely, increasingly from sheer weariness.

Much of the moor seemed lifeless. Then we'd have only the dancing bog cotton to entertain us, and the sense of higher hills solemnly watching, an occasional meadow pipit flitting ahead, chirping monotonously as if to emphasise the general silence. These Uist moors were unlike the Sutherlandshire flows where greenshanks circled piping, and red-throated divers called on every dubhlochan; or the moors of the Northern Isles, Shetland with its colonies of great skuas and terns; or Orkney where hen harriers and merlins reputedly dash at you from every patch of heath. These western island moors must be the most desolate in all Britain.

We were encouraged by patches of interest. Stonechats busy among rocks, a greenshank calling at a streamside, and a diver slipping furtively through bog bean at the edge of a loch. We found that while walking, the moor was lifeless, but if we stopped with a prospect of moorland and water, immediately we saw signs of life. A party of ravens, a family of greylag geese, a cock hen harrier beating over a shimmering level of bog cotton in flower. Once, we saw a

North Uist

party of red deer file over a distant skyline and Patricia spotted an
eagle soaring over the hill.

I began to sense the essence of the Uist moors, the quality which
distinguishes them from all other landscapes and which makes them
peculiarly attractive. 'Hauntingness' would describe it. Perception
here is less a process of active search than reflection. The moors are
something other than a sum of wildlife and views; they are a whole,
intangible atmosphere which can inflict extreme nostalgia in
absence.

Patricia summed it up rather well over lunch in the heather by
Loch Scadavay. No bird or animal to be seen, the only movement
clouds passing, the only sound water splashing among stones. Then
we grabbed binoculars to focus on a minute speck above a hill. It
was a crow. Patricia laid aside her binoculars. 'Things here always
happen at such a distance,' she said.

In the afternoon we wandered back down the convoluted east shore of Scadavay, more relaxedly now and enjoying every minute of it. We had at last adapted our pace to the moor. We strolled, stopped to examine minutiae which we would have missed earlier; lobelia flowering in the bay of the loch, wood sorrel and St John's wort on the green site of an abandoned shieling, and sunset reflected in the ruddy breastfeathering of a cock whinchat.

We must have seen enough to interest us, as we made exploratory expeditions into the moors several times during the next few weeks. The centre of the island was not uniform. Level and moist around Loch Scadavay, it changed character towards its peripheral hills and the lochs there were more sunken, stony shored. In some places, on islands in the lochs and on outcrops where sheep and deer couldn't reach them, there were even a few trees. Willows, aspen, hazel, birch, rowan; stunted and pathetic remnants of native woodland, but welcome to Patricia and me because we were accustomed to living among trees and had seen none for months.

In the middle of a raised bog, a wilderness of sedge tussocks and cotton grass – perhaps the bleakest part of the entire island – we discovered a colony of arctic skuas and were impressed by the way these birds perfectly expressed their habitat. Rapier tailed, sharp-winged, they scythed around the wide moorland sky, lifting against white cumulus or blue spaces, sweeping down to skim the levels of the moor. Their calls were ringing, challenging, keener than gulls' cries over the sea. Braving their close attacks, we found their dark brown or olive eggs laid on the shallowest scrapes in moss or peat.

We were tempted to return to the skuas, but instead went on to explore other moors in the north-east of the island. Here, we found an intricate maze of silt-based tidal inlets interset with waterlily freshwaters, of great visual beauty and quite unlike anywhere else on the island. This was moorland almost as rich in its wildlife as machair. Terns nested on flowery headlands, greylags grazed green islands, redshanks, greenshanks and curlews waded silty inlets, and more shelducks than I had ever seen bred in rabbit warrens along the shores. Common and grey seals came in with the tides and basked ecstatically on skerries. Best of all, we saw otters with cubs chasing grey mullet at the head of the tide in a secluded reed-fringed bay.

Common seal

Otter

Patricia preferred rambly, gently discursive days of exploring. She preferred level ground and didn't care for labouring steeply up-hill, so that when looking for eagles in the mountains, I usually went alone. The RSPB had supplied me with a lot of information on eagles' life-styles and habits, and a list of all the known sites in North Uist, with advice on how to find eyries of my own and approach them without unsettling the birds.

There were some half-dozen known sites, and these were checked first. None of North Uist's mountains are very high, but some of the rough moorland where eagles nested was quite remote, a long way from road or track. My researches involved miles of plodding over loch-strewn, flat bogs to reach the more upland reg-ions which are mainly along the rocky east coast. What a contrast to machairs and sand-flats, this coast where heather dropped steeply to sea cliffs, and the waters of the Minch below swirled deep and black. It was a strangely birdless coast, the cliffs unsuitable for colonies of seabirds and the moors too acid to support the small forms of life on which waders feed, and most birds of prey.

Fulmar petrels swept around some of the bays. Crows and ravens nested in the cliffs. There were colonies of rock doves which are the crofter's 'pigeons', and black guillemots wailing at me where the taller cliffs broke into ledges and caverns. Long stretches of the coast held no bird life at all and my attention was given to seals swimming below, gannets wheeling and plunging, and the coast of Skye facing me across the Minch.

On clear days I could see the grassy dome of Quirang mountain in the north of Skye, a dusting of crofts along the cliff tops of the west to Dunvegan and its lighthouse, and the distinctive shapes of Macleod's Tables to the south. But Skye was dominated by the Cuillins, a fantastic array of rocky pinnacles, still snow streaked now, in June, and constantly gathering mist and rain. An old woman who had never left the Uists once described Skye to me as 'That place of mountains and roads'. After only three months on North Uist, Skye did indeed look alien with its steep coast and mountainous skyline, leading the way to a now almost unimaginable mainland.

Behind the Minch coast of North Uist, the moors rolled back towards low heathery hills devoid of life except for small herds of red deer which moved unhurriedly out of sight. The RSPB directive assured me that eagles nested in these regions, quite a large population, supported by carrion from the deer herds and relatively intensive sheep farming. The nests were reported to be at surprisingly low levels, not necessarily on sea cliffs or the largest cliffs in the hills, but on vegetatious outcrops on the moors.

After a couple of blank days' walking, gradually I developed an eye for the eagles. They were glimpsed briefly as they drifted across a hill face or flew close to heather over a low ridge. I had to lengthen vision, take in more distant hillsides or areas of sky where a speck might be an eagle soaring. A couple of unused eyries were located, and I learned what sort of crag an eagle might use, where on the crag an eagle might be, and what the nest itself would look like from a distance.

The first occupied site was on a small but remote cleft among hills above the east coast. The hills were low in stature, but the site was a long way from the nearest road, and from the cliff there was no human habitation nearer than Skye in a view of heathery hillsides, sea and distant islands. It had a remote upland aspect. Not so the next eyrie, which was half an hour's easy stroll from the road, within sight of several croft-houses and built on a crag not much bigger than a boulder.

The first site substantiated the idea that eagles are romantic, solitary birds inhabiting lonely regions. The huge eyrie and the lofty soaring of the adult eagles seemed in keeping with the setting. The second nest aroused my protective feelings, as had the similarly accessible site shown to me by Iain. Though most crofters tolerate eagles, others do not, and if one crofter from a township is antagonistic, then any eyrie near that township is doomed. RSPB records for North Uist indicated that the accessible eyries had little chance of success. Eggs were taken or left smashed in the nest, chicks removed or destroyed. There were rumours of adult birds being shot or trapped.

Golden eagle

Now there is no doubt that a small lamb falls within the range of prey which an adult eagle is capable of taking, but my sympathies were with the eagles. Lambs have many hazards to withstand and mortality among them in the islands in extraordinarily high. Weather and terrain are against large-scale sheep rearing, and the lambs die of exposure to the cold and wet of wintry springs, and as a result of poor feeding for the ewes on acid, ill-managed moorlands. Many of the deaths among lambs are directly attributable to neglect. The flocks roam unshepherded and unfed, and the crofters' dogs, uncontrolled and half-starved, frequently attack both lambs and ewes. Sheep that die are left to rot on the hills, attracting scavengers of all kinds – ravens, gulls, crows, the township dogs. Eagles are only one of a number of potential controls to a sheep population which is far too high for this sort of ground.

It seemed wrong that eagles and other wildlife should suffer, just because crofters are encouraged by government subsidies to keep too many sheep. It was despicable that a crofter should accept a government payment readily enough, but disregard the official mandate that to persecute eagles is against the national interests. The bird protection laws which forbid the molestation of eagles hardly affected the crofters, and those who persecuted eagles refused to accept that although eagles are not uncommon in the island, they are a threatened species in Britain as a whole. A source of pleasure to an increasing number of people, the eagles of Uist might rather be regarded as a national asset than a threat to a few crofters.

Eagles had not hitherto been among my favourite birds. Of upland raptors, I preferred the speedy panache of peregrine or merlin, or the laconic grace of hen harriers. But having found a few more, previously unrecorded eyries, and evidence of one eyrie destroyed during a late, illicit heather-burning operation, I felt directly responsible for North Uist's eagles and obliged to protect them.

One of the eagles' principal apologists was a native of the island, JP and hotelier, well respected and liked. We met in the bar of his hotel, a cool shaded place on a breathless June day. He was busy with accounts but put papers and pen aside to tell of eagles, their habits, distribution and incidents of persecution. It would be difficult for me to take a firm stand in support of eagles, he advised. Uist wasn't the sort of place where legality controlled people's actions as a matter of course, and any trace of officiousness must be avoided. He wouldn't accuse anyone directly of persecuting eagles, but he gave me the name and address of someone who, he said, 'might choose to help you'. As he strolled with me to my van he advised sagely, 'Don't get worked up about it, it won't do you or the eagles any good. Take it easy.'

Holding passions in check, I went to see the clerk of a township on the west side of the island. In the past, there had been an eyrie on the hillside behind his croft, but few young eagles had been known to fledge from the nest in recent years. He was an elderly, amicable man with a shy, smiling manner. He knew of me, guessed the reason for my coming and talked readily about eagles. They were a pest, he said. One year they took thirteen of his lambs and he had seen them attacking not only his sheep but his cattle. No, he wouldn't deny that once he had been active against them; oh aye, he'd put an end to a few eaglets and adult birds, too. Not recently, however, he was getting too old for the hill and indeed he quite liked to look from the window and see an eagle soaring there. 'The tourists likes them, you know, those that comes for the beds and the breakfasts.' Besides, the old man informed me, there was a law against killing eagles now, you couldn't even smash the eggs. He hadn't been to the eyrie for years, it might still be in use. I was welcome to walk over his land and check.

The eyrie was still there and contained the remains of two eggs, smashed to bits by stones thrown from above. Standing by the little crag I looked out across the hillsides and croftlands to the machairs and sand-dunes of the Atlantic coast. It was evening, shadows lengthening – an eagle flying near would have enhanced the tranquillity of the scene.

It was hardly the best time for me to welcome eagle photographers to the island. One extremely wet morning a pair of holidaying visitors came to the caravan and in the course of general conversation mentioned that they had seen a hide on a hillside on the north coast. The couple had been merely hill-walking and had passed by without further investigation.

The hide was at an eagles' nest which had been checked recently

Eagles on the nest

and found to contain a healthy eaglet. Even without the photographers, this was a vulnerable site, close to road and township, and though eagles had once nested there regularly, this was the first time for many years that an egg had survived long enough to hatch. I had been touched by the eaglet's vigour. An upstanding little thing snapping its beak at me, dark feathers already pushing through white down, defiantly prepared to survive to maturity and yet really so helpless and endangered. Since the eyrie had been left alone so far, it might escape molestation this year and the eaglet survive. Now this photographer's hide, by all accounts a substantial, fairly conspicuous one, might draw attention to the eyrie.

I was in a quandary. Photographers are not allowed to approach eagles' nests without a special licence issued by the Nature Conservancy Council. Supplied with a list of all licences issued permitting the photography of protected birds in North Uist, as far as I knew no eagles were due to be photographed this season. Wardenship of Balranald conferred no real authority over photographers operating elsewhere on the island. It was a matter for the police or an official from the Nature Conservancy. But that would take time; meanwhile the hide would be there, advertising the presence of the eyrie.

The visitors left and I sat on in the caravan, trying to do paperwork but distracted by mental images of the hide, eyrie and distressed eagles. Resentment built up.

It was too easy for an unscrupulous photographer in North Uist to take the attitude that they could go anywhere and do anything, avoiding courtesy visits announcing his or her intentions to landowners or the local RSPB warden. So I brooded. At about four in the afternoon, I couldn't concentrate at all and pushed aside pens and paper and drove through the sledging rain to the north of the island – anything to relieve frustration and complete inaction.

Labouring in waterproofs through long heather, I climbed the hillside opposite and scanned across with binoculars and telescope. The hide was a few yards from the nest on which sat the eaglet, a white dot. The adult eagles were absent. It is typical behaviour at this stage for the adults to be away from the nest for long periods, returning no more than twice a day to bring prey to the eaglet. In all the rain and mist the surrounding hills and valley, a pleasant spot on a sunny day, were now a drear place of rain-wet scree and boulder, dark heather, streams foaming where none had existed before.

I plodded across to the eyrie, took a look at the eaglet which cowered miserably under a slight overhang, and inside the empty hide. It had been erected with some care, guy ropes secured into cracks in the rock. Suddenly, irrationally, I was angry. To go away and leave this canvas monstrosity here would be a weakness, an abrogation of responsibility. After all, there was no one on North Uist to take the eagles' part.

I unpegged the hide, folded the canvas, gathered pegs and ropes together and carried the lot down to my van. Slinging it in the back I drove home, feeling self-righteous, but nervously anxious about possible consequences.

It was getting dark now. Passing the gateway to The Glebe, Iain appeared dimly through unceasing rain, waving me to a halt. He jumped into the passenger seat. 'You can take me up to The Glebe,' he announced. 'Someone's been phoning you, wants you to ring back immediately.'

Cursing a presumed birdwatcher anxious to arrange a visit to the reserve, I went dripping into The Glebe and rang the number Mary had written down for me. It was my acquaintance the hotelier and eagle enthusiast.

'Thought I'd better keep you informed,' his voice came urbanely over the phone. 'There's a film unit on the island, sent by some conservation organisation to get material on certain rare birds.'

'Have they got licences?' I asked, painfully.

'Oh, I should think so. They could hardly risk it without, could they? It would be bad for their image. I particularly thought you ought to know since apparently they have a hide up on an eagle.'

A weakness overcame me. I put a steadying hand on Mary's table and saw my oilskin sleeve still spattered with rain. 'I've just this minute taken the bloody thing down.'

There was a thoughtful silence at the other end. The sort of silence that occurs when a dignified person smiles quietly to himself and strokes a long chin.

'I think I'd better give you their address.' He gave it, a croft-house in the south of the island. 'You have my number, haven't you? Do give me a ring in a day or two, let me know how you got on. And, ah, the best of luck. I'm sure you feel in need of it.'

In The Glebe kitchen, I blurted out the whole story to the Macdonalds. Mary clucked her tongue, Murdo was non-committal, Iain was delighted. 'Serve you right, none of your business. I suppose you'll really be in trouble now.' He did a gleeful little dance at the other side of the table, then stopped, noticing my expression. Instantly he was serious. 'Don't take it hard, man. Look, if I go with you now we could put their tent or whatever it is up again. Nobody would know.'

It might indeed have worked. The kindness of Iain's offer almost brought tears, but I couldn't take him away from his home so late, on such a night. Refusing Mary's offer of a meal, I left The Glebe and drove south through the pouring darkness.

When I found the cottage where the film unit was staying and knocked hesitantly at the door, it didn't help at all that the chief cameraman should be immediately welcoming. The warden of Balranald, how good it was of me to call.

The _Seven Sisters_, a local creel boat

147

Unable to just stand there, making puddles in his porch and exchanging pleasantries, I steeled myself to say: 'Your hide, the one you have erected on the eagle's eyrie.'

'Yes?' He raised his eyebrows, surprised.

'It's in my van, outside.' He was extremely angry. As he warmed to his invective against ignorant meddling conservationists he became apoplectic, finally incoherent.

'I was going there tomorrow. The first day of filming. Look, I've just finished making up my sandwiches for the day.' He was a stubby little man with a bald crown up and down which his eyebrows leaped as if they'd break free and fly away. His already protuberant eyes bulged like headlamps and a sweat of wrath broke on his jowls. His words fought for clarity with rage and a thickening North Country accent.

'Luke 'ere, yer booger, joost luke 'ere.' He waved at me a sandwich box which contained an apple, a large pork pie and a tin of sardines. His rage made me calm but no longer apologetic.

'I do think you might have contacted me. You're in the islands now, where people haven't yet forgotten what simple courtesy means.'

There might have been an ugly scene, but the other member of the film unit intervened. He explained that they had not received licences until recently and were left with no time for the usual formalities. He apologised to me now, and the good manners of this assistant cameraman had a generally calming effect.

We all went through to the sitting-room and, among all the scattered paraphernalia of the film business, we sat down to talk it out. Now and then the head cameraman threatened to become violently angry again, but that assistant was a true diplomat. He made tea, offered it formally on a tray. 'Sugar? Two? A little milk?' We couldn't maintain aggressiveness. The assistant also supplied the ideal solution. He would take the unit car and we two would go to the eyrie now and reinstate the hide. Then the filming could proceed as planned.

Machair: a flat strip of fertile land between sea and wilderness and (below) an eagle chick on the nest, defenceless against the persecution which threatens the survival of the island's eagle population

The foul weather broke, moonlight silvered wet rocks as we marched the hide back to the eyrie, carefully re-erected it and walked back to the road. I stumbled, had eaten nothing since lunch, and was exhausted. The assistant sat with me in the wet heather and from his rucksack produced a slab of chocolate and an orange. We at the chocolate and then the orange slice by slice in turn, off the top of a rock. Energy came back. We talked of birds and birding, and the moon shone on the sea and islands in the Sound of Harris. A wren called in the heather and a curlew's note came from the croft-land. Soon it would be the morning of a beautiful day. I may not have merited his goodwill but that cameraman was a generous, gracious man, and when we reached our vehicles at the roadside we shook hands, parted as friends.

Next day I went to see my eagle-loving friend at his hotel. His judgement of the affair was lenient. 'You were impetuous, it's true. But you might have achieved some good in the long term. No future eagle photographer will fail to contact the warden at Balranald.'

Comforted, in a day or two my protective passion for eagles had to be shared with phalaropes. One of Britain's rarest birds, a species for which Balranald was particularly celebrated, they arrived to nest on the reserve.

Red-necked phalaropes had caught my imagination when, as a boy, I had read a long article about them in one of my father's or-nithological magazines. The author described how he had made an expedition to certain western islands of Scotland especially to see the species, and after a certain amount of searching and encounter with other unusual birds and even more unusual people, he had

(pp150–1) On rare still days the lochs form mirrors for impressive skies

A fence stretches across Loch Paible expressing the timeless beauty of the island

Red-necked phalarope (female)

come across a colony of phalaropes on some shallow freshwater loch on a remote island. It might well have been North Uist and Loch nam Feithean in the 1920s. The engaging things about the phalaropes were firstly their rarity, then the extraordinarily confiding behaviour of the birds. They would spin and paddle at your feet, and would even sit on their eggs in your hand.

The bird was composed of oddities. It was a wader but it swam like a duck, and its typical behaviour was to spin round and round in tight circles, like some clockwork bath toy; whether in courtship display or as a method of feeding, the author couldn't say. Unlike most British birds, the female phalarope took the initiative in courtship and was the more brightly plumaged of the pair, while the male took over the business of incubation and rearing the young.

Phalaropes were just too eccentric to be common, and somehow their oddity suited their occurrence only in the extreme north and west of Britain. They were, however, reputedly plentiful enough in northern Scandinavia, Iceland and Greenland where they formed breeding colonies of up to a dozen pairs on a single stretch of water. The author of my boyhood article wrote of rowing his island loch and dipping his oars among phalaropes as they bobbed by his boat.

Since the 1920s of the article, phalaropes had become even rarer as a British bird. They had disappeared from many areas, and colonies in places where they had once been plentiful had now shrunk to a few pairs. There were now virtually no phalaropes on the Scottish mainland, a drastically reduced number in the Western Isles, and the British stronghold was now certain uninhabited islands in the Shetlands. At the time of my Balranald wardenship, phalaropes had not nested successfully on the reserve for several years. Last season they had not attempted to breed at all, and it was now doubtful if they bred regularly anywhere in North Uist.

Opinion about the necessity for protecting phalaropes in Britain was divided. Some said they should be preserved, others that Britain was on the limit of their breeding range and there was no urgent need for protection while the species thrived elsewhere. Neither school offered any reason for the decline of phalaropes in Britain: a natural fluctuation of a fringe population, alteration or disappearance of habitat, increased predation – nobody seemed to know. I didn't presume to supply answers or even hold an informed opinion about their protection, but they promised to be intriguing, engaging birds, and I merely hoped that while at Balranald, I would see something of them.

A watchful eye was kept on the shallow lagoons of Loch nam Feithean and on its broad sandy-bottomed bays. All other wading birds preferred these areas which, as May drew towards June, were a delight to the human eye. Bog-bean flourished, pushing out thick green mats from the loch edge and sending up spires of pinkish white flowers. In the lush vegetation of the banks grew many orchids, including the lilac, early spotted, and the more robust, deeply purple columns of the northern marsh variety. Cresses, including delectable edible watercress, thrived with water forget-me-not, watermint, brooklime, and marsh willow-herb in creeks and old ditches. Rushes lengthened and formed dense stands where a month ago the water was open, and amphibious bistort made rafts out on the surface, red flowerheads just beginning to show.

Eels sinuated through tangled waterweeds, aqueous thickets of common pondweeds, stonewort and milfoil. Water beetles rowed themselves endlessly up and down. Skaters pitted a still surface like rain and every morning and evening feeding trout made slow circles. There were dragonflies, damselflies, wandering bees seeking a change from clover and charlock on the machair; clusters of diptera and beetles on burgeoning hogweeds and other umbelliferae;

Dunlin

and iris in damp patches standing tall as miniature woodland.

Gulls and terns hawked around, curlews stooped elegantly to bathe, herons gorged themselves on the eels. I examined many hundreds of dunlin with exaggerated care, and a swimming redshank once almost deceived me. Every other sort of wader and waterbird visited these wildlife-congested marshland bays, but May came to its close and still the phalaropes did not appear.

One morning in early June I left Loch nam Feithean after failing again to find phalaropes, and wandered disconsolately over the fields towards Hougharry. It was very early, sunny and calm, pale-washed after a night of rain. Lapwing chicks ran among the daisies, and old MacIsaac and his wife, a crofting couple from the township, came across the field together to milk and tether their cow. Phalaropes or not it was an idyllic Uist tableau: MacIsaac leading the cow with a hempen rope loosely around its neck to another patch of buttercups and stooping to bang in the tethering peg with his hammer; his aproned wife settling herself at the cow's side with her pail, Gaelic voices coming wind-brought over the field, the houses of Hougharry beyond and morning sunlight on the sea.

I liked the MacIsaacs; like phalaropes they were a type declining even in Uist. I idled over to join them in contemplation of the cow. He was small and thin with a highly pitched voice and he had not only the accent but the island manner of speech: the wandering of words round meanings like water adapting itself to stones, the occasional swift cadence. His wife was taller, stout, her face whiskered and weathered, and she was noted for her loud shrieking voice. Iain once said of her, 'you can hear Ellie MacIsaac whispering from Hougharry to the Ard'. She shrieked at me that morning, like one of the gulls I'd just been watching on the marsh.

'Here, come here. I want to speak to you.' It was her husband who broke the news. He was very excited, and since English was for him a second language, it wasn't easy to understand what he said. One of those birds, the sort people came to see and the wardens were always asking about, he'd seen one last night while he was out at the cow. No, not a corncrake; a bird that sat on the water, he'd seen it just over there in the loch, near the village.

I left them quickly and walked over the field to an insignificant patch of water which almost disappears in drought and into which the villagers throw a lot of unsightly rubbish. This season had been wet, the loch was full, with a rushy fringe and a reedy bay with a small island at one end.

A knoll above this bay overlooked the whole loch, which had no creek or indentation where a bird even as small as a phalarope might be concealed. A farm track ran alongside the loch, field fences came to the water's edge, hens from the nearest house in Hougharry habitually bathed in it and basked on the bank. Compared to Loch nam Feithean it was a disturbed and unlovely stretch of water, but I scrutinised it meticulously, every inch of water and bank. A mallard family was shuttling about in the rushes, disturbed by a collie which came to drink, eyed me, and trotted away with tail defiantly erect. A common gull sat on its nest on the island and two ringed plovers were pleeping foolishly on a strip of shingle. I sat there for half an hour and closely scanned that miserable pond perhaps twenty times. There was not a phalarope to be seen.

Convinced that no phalaropes were present, I walked to the edge of the reedy bay. There, midway between bank and island, in full view about a yard from my feet, a little bird sat buoyantly on the water. It chirped, jerked a foot forward, span a rapid perfect circle and sat again in the ripples of its spinning. It wasn't possible, but it was indubitably a female phalarope in full breeding plumage.

The loch was suddenly the most attractive stretch of water in the world. I didn't question the phalarope, only marvelled as it span again and again, made rapid flights across the loch, came back to the same place, preened, dabbled, swam to within a foot of me – too close for me to focus binoculars on it – and chirped a clear, peremptory note. Every movement it made was graceful and it wasn't still for a second. Everything about it from sharp wing-tip to hair-fine bill was refined to a point of evanescence. It might appear like a Celtic fairy from nowhere and vanish again as bewilderingly. It seemed agonisingly at the limit of human apprehension, spinning there.

Red-necked phalarope

This first phalarope did not vanish. She attracted a mate, a beautiful little creature in himself but dominated by the female's more urgently active manner, his delicate plumage colouring eclipsed by her brightness. Never before had the dingy loch been so constantly watched by the Balranald warden. A little later another pair of phalaropes moved into the lagoon area of Loch nam Feithean as first expected, and there seemed hope that this season might vindicate Balranald's declining reputation as a phalarope sanctuary.

The two pairs made contact, as befitted a species which normally breeds in colonies. One day there were five phalaropes, three females and two males, in a pool below Goular cemetery, and they put on a display of incomparable avian joie de vivre. They were eye-deceivingly fast in flight, but more buoyant than butterflies. They had the same robust waterbird exuberance of a teal, yet they were the most elegant of waders. Among the three female birds, the lady from the township loch was conspicuous, more contrastingly coloured than the others; her white face patches were immaculate, her neck feathers plushed out into a vivid crimson ruff. She was my first love, I was truly infatuated.

Between the two lochs I scuttled obsessively, binoculars and notebook in hand, until convinced that the township loch male was sitting on eggs on the island in the bay and the other male was incubating in a more secluded, infinitely more attractive site at Loch nam Feithean. Then the female birds disappeared to go courting elsewhere, or, with their breeding season finished, out to ocean whence they came. I settled patiently to wait and watch over my two now inconspicuous and broody males.

Birdwatchers arrived at my caravan in increasing numbers as the summer wore on. Most wanted to see the reserve birds, the phalaropes, and this presented me with a problem. The two sitting male birds showed themselves only rarely and in the immediate vicinity of their nests. How were sightings for visitors to be arranged without disturbing the birds or betraying the whereabouts of their nest sites? The visitors seemed genuine, usually likable enthusiasts, but I was wary of egg collectors, or photographers who might press their attentions too close. I decided to keep the township site secret and advise people to watch the shore of Loch nam Feithean from Goular cemetery. Most people were satisfied with this, and if they failed to sight phalaropes, they were happy with corncrakes, other waders and seabirds.

Because people were asked not to walk through the sensitive marsh, an alternative route must be offered, and an informal 'nature trail' was devised across the machair to Ard an Runair, around the coast of the headland and back across Hougharry Bay. This route enabled people to see a fair selection of the habitats of the reserve: machair, sand-dunes, beaches and headland, and they could see enough of the freshwater marshes from a viewpoint in Goular cemetery or the road passing by Loch nam Feithean on the way to the caravan.

In those days many RSPB reserves maintained a permit system for visitors whereby the visitor assured himself of his day's birding and the wardening staff knew when to expect him. Conducted tours were arranged, hides provided or guidance offered by noticeboards and information leaflets. At Balranald, all such organisation was inappropriate. With an average of a thousand or so birdwatching visitors every season, it was one of the least visited of all the society's reserves; hides and other elaborate means of controlling and advising people were considered unnecessary. The society did not own the land at Balranald and could not restrict access, so there could be no days of closure, no official control of times for visiting, no forbidden areas. I had no real authority to restrict access to the marshes or keep people to my nature trail, but could only appeal to common sense and sympathy, and hope that people would be satisfied with the minimal guidance provided.

Visitors arrived unannounced at any time of day, knocked on the door of the caravan hoping that the warden would be at home. I had much fieldwork to do, work on the cottage, and I needed a certain amount of personal privacy. So a noticeboard was improvised giving information about birds and other natural history features, directing people to the nature trail, asking them to refrain from entering the marshes and generally conduct themselves in accordance with the nature reserve status of the place. That noticeboard was a mixture of tact and unlawfully assumed authority. It was also very large, painted a conspicuous blue and erected some little distance from the caravan. I hoped that it would keep the majority of visitors away from my door.

On the whole I was fortunate with my visitors. In the early part of the summer, most of the people were genuine enthusiasts, prepared to pay high ferry charges and risk uncertain weather to see Uist and its birds. They were themselves amateur conservationists, sympathetic to the aims of the society and anxious to comply with instructions.

Almost without exception they behaved impeccably and as the season passed their visits fell into an ideal pattern. A party arrived from guest-house or hotel at mid-morning. Leaving their cars by the noticeboard they took birdwatching equipment and packed lunches off on the nature trail. Following the route slowly and not too strictly they wandered over the machair, noticing its flowers, to the beach at Traigh Iar where there were always birds to be seen. Everyone, birdwatcher or not, responds to a sweep of oceanic strand. Ard an Runair gave easy walking among splendid scenery, with seabirds and on clear days the thrilling sight of St Kilda to the west, the mountains of Harris in the north. An ideal visitor would walk slowly, be moved by the scene as much as by the birdlife, potter among shingly beaches and sea pools, admire the terns at a respectful distance and take a long lunch-break among thrift and thyme, piping oystercatchers and ringed plovers.

Hougharry Bay supplied more waders, more fascinating rock and sand pools, hard-ribbed sands for striding and loose sun-warmed sand and dune for barefoot dawdling. Sunburned, wind-ruffled and happy; visitors would be back at their car by mid-afternoon. A perfect finish to the day was a peaceful session in the cemetery, telescopes and binoculars trained on the marshes. They could spend an hour or more actively birdwatching or in contemplation of the scene. Some birdwatchers went to the cemetery in the afternoon and lingered there, among tombstones and moths and corncrakes, until dark.

Oystercatcher

I blessed that cemetery and the crofters who allowed visitors so freely to stroll or sit among their respected dead. Part of the cemetery was still in use, and on days when funeral services were held my birdwatchers were warned by means of an addition to the noticeboard. There must be no recreational use of the cemetery those days, when a procession arrived from the kirk, and an all-male body of islanders shouldered a coffin up the path between gravestones. Solemn days. Bareheaded darkly clad men grouped around the open grave while the minister's voice mingled with the wind and the cries of disturbed lapwings. Funerals happened surprisingly often, sometimes two or three a week, and it seemed that the local population must be rapidly dwindling. But Uist people are as healthy as people anywhere, and in fact there is a tendency for them not to die in the summer. Like a cow or sheep, if you survived a winter you were expected to last through to October at least. But exiled relatives often expressed the wish to be returned to the island when they died. Goular cemetery with its wide prospect of machair, marsh and sea was particularly popular and a high proportion of the crofters who arrived shoulder-borne to Goular had started their journey in America or Canada.

When working away from the caravan area, my usual time for making contact with visitors was towards evening when they returned from their walk around the headland. Then I enjoyed discussion of what they had seen, and often went with them for their final session in the cemetery. These meetings were informal, they gave the visitors a personal contact which they seemed to value, and for me they constituted an agreeable substitute for a more conventional social life.

Some visitors paid only one visit to the reserve. Others fell for the place and came repeatedly, and with some of these an acquaintance was made for the duration of their holiday. I might offer a conducted tour, or suggest that they accompany me on a day's fieldwork, or take a holiday myself to go birdwatching with them away from the reserve.

One couple were on vacation from university jobs in Aberdeen. Having lived a while in Aberdeen myself, I enjoyed hearing again the warm, rapid, Aberdeen dialect, and found the people agreeable as the Aberdonians of my past. They particularly endeared themselves to me because they didn't demand to see phalaropes or other rarities, didn't even insist on corncrakes. They were interested in waders, they said, and what they most wanted from this holiday trip was to see a nest of a common redshank. The man was apologetic. He didn't want to cause me too much trouble, but he hadn't found a redshank's nest since as a boy he had rambled through rushy fields by the Aberdeenshire Dee. There were no rushes in those fields now, no springtime redshanks.

I couldn't think offhand of the precise location of a nest, but there was no shortage either of rushy fields or redshanks at Balranald. From where we stood talking we could hear a dozen song-flighting over the marshes. I led the pair to the margin of Loch nam Feithean, and there on a dry grassy bank we sat and watched. Redshanks, snipe and lapwings circled round us. It was difficult to concentrate on one bird among so many, but gradually the agitation died down.

With binoculars I followed one redshank in its lower and lower circlings until it landed, ran a dozen yards and vanished among dense ditchside umbelliferae. Still watching the precise spot, I asked the woman to walk towards it. She did so, treading carefully over the marshy ground. As she neared the spot where the redshank had disappeared the bird flew up again, yelping alarm, from slightly deeper into the marsh. Concentrating fully on this second spot I gestured the woman towards it. A little to the right, a little further; she stood by the exact tussock, waving delightedly for us to come and see.

There were four olive, brown-mottled eggs in a bower of rushes, a pair of redshanks complaining over our heads. The man took a photograph and we withdrew, leaving the birds to resettle. I affected nonchalance, as if finding nests was something I could do anytime, on request; actually I was as pleased and more surprised by my instant success than were my visitors.

They were impressed and grateful. After that they came to the reserve daily, and if I was out left a note at the door, more than once with some gift – a jar of coffee, a bag of apples. One evening they made a find which excited them even more than my lucky redshank's nest. I met them on the machair.

'Did you see it then?' asked the man.

'See what?'

Snowy owl

'Why, the big white bird, you must have walked right past it.'

I thought, 'Oh no, not another stranded gannet.'

'It's a snowy owl, you've got one on the reserve, not half a mile from your door.'

I didn't believe it, thinking that he must have spotted a short-eared owl, pale brown owls which often hunted the marshes at evening. But I followed them along the farm track and looked through binoculars at the white object they indicated, shapeless and at a distance dismissible as a plastic farm bag, lying close to one of the machair fences. It was a snowy owl, a pure white adult male, mantling over a dead rabbit and using the wire fence as protection from the wildly mobbing waders. When it shrank back into its feathers it looked almost headless, corpulent as a seal; when a lapwing flew near, it unsheathed a powerful hooked bill and made a hiss that we could hear a hundred yards away.

Back at the caravan the Aberdonians accepted tea and delivered their latest gift, a packet of shortbreads. A small celebration, and some amusement at my expense. At least three times that day I must have passed unnoticingly within a hundred yards of that huge stark white bird, probably the only snowy owl in Britain south of the Shetlands. That would take some living down among birdwatching circles, no matter how many redshanks' nests were casually found!

We were convinced that the owl was a vagrant and would probably leave when it had eaten its rabbit, perhaps during the night. But it stayed. It moved from the machair and took up a stance on a wall top at the edge of the marshes and was still on the reserve when the Aberdonians left at the end of their holiday. It stayed on and on incredibly through the summer, from June to September.

A snowy owl which insisted on displaying itself a few hundred yards from the road was something which couldn't be kept secret. Very soon the news had spread that a birdwatcher at Balranald might see the owl in addition to regular attractions like corncrakes and phalaropes, and rarity hunters arrived from all over Britain.

Just at this time another extremely rare bird put in an appearance on a beach in South Uist. This was a Steller's eider, an American duck previously recorded in Britain only a few times. It was a drake of the species, in breeding plumage, sufficient in itself to attract those birdwatchers who specialise in scarce vagrants. Coupled with the snowy owl at Balranald, it caused an unprecedented focusing of interest on the Western Isles.

Steller's eider duck

The rarity hunters have an elitist clique which bases its activities on the north coast of Norfolk. The Norfolk marshes are their home ground, but they will travel inordinate distances to ratify occurrences of vagrant birds, and now a rumour reached me that some of these people intended to charter an aeroplane and fly out to the Uists. The flight plan failed, but a group did arrive by car and they travelled bird-spotting from Lochboisdale in South Uist, via the Steller's eider towards Balranald's snowy owl.

I was mildly apprehensive. These fanatics must be prevented from trampling over the marshes, disturbing phalaropes and other birds in an attempt to get close to the owl. There was no need to worry. The group arrived at evening and camped decorously in a crofter's field close to the reserve. At a considerable hour next morning they walked to the caravan, intent on contacting the warden before trying to find the bird. They looked strange, a mixture of the outrageous and unlikely. One girl wore pink overalls, a floppy cowboy hat and climbing boots. Around her slender neck hung the largest, heaviest pair of binoculars I had ever seen. They looked as if they should be mounted on the deck of a ship or coin operated by tourists on a holiday resort pier. Leadership of the group was divided between herself and a gentleman in a plush-collared black overcoat, white shirt and tie, elegant tapered flannels and polished town shoes. He wore a grey trilby with pheasant's feather and smoked cheroots.

The rest of the party showed a high incidence of lank hair and beards, but the most pronounced common feature of the group was an over sufficiency of expensive equipment: binoculars, telescopes, cameras, tripods, devices for sound recording and at least one portable hide.

However determined the group or improbable their appearance, their behaviour at Balranald was impeccable. They sat in the cemetery for several hours, studying their owl and making meticulous notes, and they did the regulation walk around my nature trail without showing any inclination to trespass in search of more exciting species. They didn't see the phalaropes which were incubating firmly, but before they left the reserve they gathered at the caravan to thank me, and many pushed coins into the RSPB's collection box at the door.

The group from Norfolk represented the specialist, almost professional element among rare bird enthusiasts. Their behaviour contrasted with that of a 16-year-old I found wandering in the marsh one day under a cloud of disturbed birds. I ejected him and a couple of hours later found him again, this time trying to force an approach through the reed-beds at Paible. When he saw me bearing down on him he ran, but came back a third time, at dusk, when I caught him trying to sneak past the caravan towards the cemetery. I

166

was curious now as well as angry, and, dragging him inside out of the rain, cursed him soundly and gave him a mug of tea. He had hoped, he confessed, to sleep in the cemetery, see the snowy owl by the first light of morning, and get away without being noticed. But why hadn't he made a conventional approach, which would have enabled him to see his bird without all this furtive behaviour and inconvenience to himself and me?

'I didn't think you'd let me see it; people don't generally let me do anything.' What a background of deprivation he must have suffered, this schoolboy from London. I couldn't totally condemn him, he had shown initiative and determination, and his energy was unbelievable. On his way to Balranald, he had phoned friends in London who reported a western sandpiper, a very rare wader, as present on an estuary in Essex. So he had boarded the next ferry, hitchhiked to Essex, 'ticked off' the sandpiper, and hitchhiked back to North Uist for the owl – all in ten days. No wonder he looked gaunt and hollow-eyed. I allowed him to sleep in the RSPB cottage, and arranged to conduct him to the snowy owl in the morning. At 8 o'clock next morning the door of the cottage was swinging open, the birdwatcher gone, and I never knew whether or not he managed to see the snowy owl.

Snowy owl

My favourite of all the birdwatching visitors that season was a pair of elderly ladies, retired schoolmistresses from Lancashire. They came in July, by which time I had started my renovations of the cottage, and on the morning of their arrival was up on the roof, happily Snowcemming the stone chimney. The car drew up, the ladies consulted the noticeboard and I hoped they would follow its instructions without trying to contact me. It was an awkward moment, the roof was steep and none too safe, and my grip precarious. I wanted to finish with the minimum of climbing up and down and had one side of the chimney, perhaps a quarter of an hour's work, to complete.

The ladies looked up from the noticeboard, saw me on the roof, and walked across. I waved a white brush cheerfully in greeting. 'You will excuse me, won't you, if I don't come down this minute. I shall be with you in less than half an hour, or if you'd care to make a start on the nature trail . . .'

The ladies regarded me severely. One of them removed her spectacles. 'Young man, we have driven several hundreds of miles and made a sea journey, with the express purpose of meeting you and seeing this reserve. I am 78 and my companion Edith is 74. We have been members of the RSPB for more than two decades. Now I do think you might spare a moment for a few words.'

I laid aside brush and paint and came down from the roof as quickly as possible. They were not to be fobbed off with noticeboards and guide-yourself nature trails, this pair; they had visited reserves with sophisticated arrangements for visitors, and were regulars to their local reserve, Leighton Moss in Lancashire.

'We know your warden there, Mr Wilson, very well. He always meets us when we make our permit visits, and once he even took us himself to see water-rails.'

Nothing for it. I could hardly allow Balranald to be compared unfavourably with Leighton Moss, or myself considered less welcoming than Mr Wilson. We set off together for Ard an Runair.

It turned into one of the happiest day's birdwatching of my career. We started with mixed waders at Traigh Iar and moved through arctic terns to shelducks and eiders with ducklings among the rocks of Ard an Runair. At lunch in a flowery niche on the headland we saw manx shearwaters and gannets, and an obliging diver in

Manx shearwater

Hougharry Bay helped the ladies overcome tiredness during the last mile.

The pair had an immense capacity to enjoy everything. They were like children; experienced birdwatchers though they were, their appreciation was not jaded by any preconceived idea of what birds were more typically Hebridean than others; and rarity had no special appeal. A common lapwing was as much a source of delight as any exotic vagrant strayed to the beach. They were absorbed for an hour watching a seal and passionately interested when we found otter tracks on the hard sand of Hougharry Bay. They were as attentive to information about the crofting way of life as they were eager to learn about birds. Had nothing else engaged their attentions they would have been perfectly happy with the scenery, the splendid weather of the day. Schoolmistresses to the frail bone though they were, their vitality and old-fashioned charm made their company delightful.

I sat with the ladies for an hour in the cemetery, listening to corncrakes and pointing out the marshland birds, then invited them to tea in the caravan. All trace of school-spinsterish hauteur removed by the outdoor day, once inside the caravan they became girlish. They considered my domestic arrangements primitive and extremely funny. 'All these tins of baked beans, you must have an exceptional liking for them.' I'd never thought about it. You bought food, you bought baked beans, you could heat them up or spoon them cold from the tin. Not a question of liking. Now I considered the tins ranked on my shelf. 'In fact, I dislike baked beans, extremely.' The ladies shrieked with laughter. They became gay; they confiscated my teatowels for washing, they twittered conspiratorily out to their car and came back with a box from which they made a delicious omelette for three. By the time we reached the stage of coffee and fruit, we were friends unreservedly laughing together and exchanging personal confidences. A short walk round Ard an Runair, but it crossed a gap of fifty years, the difference between my age and theirs.

Every day of their fortnight's holiday the ladies went birdwatching, walking, sightseeing in different parts of the Uists and Benbecula. Every evening they came to see me and we discussed what they had seen during the day. I looked forward to their evening visit when we would all sit cosily cramped in the caravan, around their notebooks open on the table. On their last evening they were escorted to see phalaropes, and the male at Loch nam Feithean obliged, hawking tern-like after insects over the still water of the lagoon. That evening the ladies cooked me another meal which we ate by candlelight, and when they drove away I watched until the red tail lights of their car vanished among dark hills. I had become accustomed to solitude, but for some weeks afterwards evenings without the ladies seemed rather lonely.

Another visiting couple accompanied me on an outing to the offshore island of Causamul which is part of the Balranald bird reserve. For me it was a work trip. I had to go to census the birds, but the company of this pair would make an interesting task even more of a pleasure. Causamul lies 5 miles by boat from Hougharry across the bay and round the headland. It is less than a mile long, 1/4 mile at its widest and only 30ft from sea to summit. For its size, Causamul supports a surprising number and variety of seabirds, and it also has notable colonies of grey and common seals. Wave-smothered all winter, it is more of a skerry than an island, and its vegetation is that of a true Atlantic outlier, consisting only of plants which can resist submergence and salt spray even during a short flowering season, and heavy liming from the seabirds' summer colonies.

No grass grows on Causamul, only seaweed and lichen on the lower rocks, and scentless mayweed and scurvy grass on shingly parts of the shore. The upper rocks are bare of vegetation but plastered white by the seabirds' droppings; seen from Ard an Runair on a warm July day this coating of guano makes Causamul a fiction, a fragment of Tir-nan-Og, legendary island utopia where snow lies in midsummer.

Cormorant

Causamul certainly looked enchanting as we approached it by lobster boat across blue-green, bow-slapping Atlantic. It was a soft, sunny summer's day, the sea was puppy-like, harmlessly playful. It might have been a gingerbread island, lichenous rocks sun-warmed to the colour of cake, generously dusted with sugar. But it was neither myth nor edible. We jumped awkwardly from the boat onto the slippery rocks, and the sudden stench of seabirds almost choked us. Causamul was inhabited not by wee folk in diaphanous clothes, but by thousands of very real and now disturbed birds. The smell was disgusting, the noise tremendous.

The lobster boat chugged off towards creels set round the Monach Islands. The crew of Hougharry fishermen gave us a derisive cheer. They had said they would leave us for nine hours, coming back when a rising tide cleared the dangerous rocks. I had readily agreed but now watching the boat go wondered if we would survive nine hours in this place. Bad enough for me, relatively accustomed to close contact with birds; it must be agony for my guests.

Sitting as near to the sea as possible on the windward side of the island, after a while the smell was less offensive. While acclimatising, we watched the birds, mainly vast flocks of cormorants and shags which had left their nests and now sat together a short distance out to sea. The gulls were less patient; they didn't gather to wait for us to leave but wheeled around the island, a blizzard of gulls and every one of them seeming to scream a note of dissent with the rest. Occasionally a herring gull or huge intimidating black-back detached itself from the general mêlée and swept to within feet of our heads. At first we ducked, then we realised that gulls, unlike terns, were unlikely to strike us, and ignored the attacks. The terns were on the other side of the island, already resettled on their nests in the shingle and I didn't intend to disturb them.

A few puffins whirred by, squawking protest although their beaks were filled with fish, and black guillemots swam and dived below us rowing themselves underwater with their white-patched wings like water beetles in an outsize pond. Only the fulmar petrels and the seals showed no fear and no aggression. The seals were like fishermen's floats painted by a child to simulate human beings – domed bobbing heads, perfectly circular dark eyes – while the fulmars alone among the birds were silent, never interrupting their

Puffins

endless gliding to attack us. They were perpetually watchful and we felt more menace in their silence than in any of the other birds' noisy display.

There were so many nests on the island that it was impossible to count them precisely. I tried to move systematically, exhausting one area before moving on to the next, in an attempt to make a reasonably accurate estimation of numbers. Some places had to be missed simply because we couldn't place our feet between the gulls' nests, and it was important to avoid disturbing the arctic tern colony since, if the adult terns were distracted, the gulls would certainly swoop in and eat their eggs and young. It was possible to walk through the shag and cormorant colonies counting nests and the hideous young, though these areas ran wet with fresh guano and the smell was indescribable. I worked quickly, then we all moved to

173

Puffin in flight

the top of the island, an instinctive impulse to find fresh air. It was worse on the top: the gulls pressed their attacks more closely and now we were threatened by the fulmars below; not by the adult petrels – they still wheeled impassively by – but by the chicks which sat in a dense colony around the island cairn. These little monsters were all beak and belly. As we passed they stabbed at our legs and vomited the contents of their well-stocked crops at us with astonishing force and accuracy. This defensive adaptation is particularly offensive in fulmars; the regurgitated substance (euphemised as 'oil') smells worse than merely decaying or half-digested sicked-up fish. It has a nauseous musky quality of its own. It is also difficult to remove. Visit a fulmar colony and you have to pumice your skin afterwards and burn all your clothes.

The St Kildans might have subsisted on fulmar and gannet chicks stewed in their own oil, but they also relished ancient eggs and their stomachs were probably as singular as St Kildan housemice and wrens. The fulmar chicks of Causamul made us skip and retch as we stepped between them to examine the cairn, white as a Snow-cemmed OS trig point, plastered evenly with inches of guano.

Of all the inhabitants of Causamul, the topmost tenants of this avian slum were the most astonishing. They were starlings – birds of towns, parks, gardens – the same birds which flocked to roost on buildings or in high trees over farmland; everyone's bird

174

neighbour, quite at home here on Causamul among gulls and guano, nesting in rock crannies around the cairn.

The starlings had found a place here, but I found Causamul totally hostile. Exciting, even exhilarating, but there could be no peace with the place so disturbed by my presence, when every step caused a fresh storm of protest. My guests were similarly affected. They were interested, at times incredulous, but after looking briefly at the cairn we withdrew as far as possible from the true possessors, the birds, and spent the remainder of our visit on low-tide rocks.

With several hundred yards between us and the nearest nesting birds, we found a relative calm. The sea slapped against rocks, the seals gathered close by to watch us with their big solemn eyes and behind us the commotion gradually quietened. They were peaceful creatures, the seals. Causamul attracts both British species, com-

Fulmar

Arctic terns

mon seals to raise pups in the spring, grey seals in groups for some reason called rookeries, to begin their breeding season in autumn. It was easy to distinguish the smaller round-headed common variety from the long-nosed greys.

'I prefer the common ones,' pronounced the lady. 'Those grey ones, they are more like horses.' People of the sea and their long-nosed horses, there might be a legend in the simile, if she'd care to invent one. In Gaelic mythology the seals, common or grey, are always people or the souls of people, sometimes sirening humans away to join them at sea. Seals on land, or humans in a seal's world, the legends never allow either to rest in the other's element for long.

The midsummer part of the season was a hectic time. Days of ornithological field-work alternated with sessions of paperwork, trying to reach conclusions about bird distribution, habitat and the general condition of the reserve. This was in preparation for summarising reports to be compiled from the mass of dats and impression gathered during the birds' breeding season. A score or so birdwatchers came to the reserve daily, all expecting individual, personal attention, and whenever time could be spared and the weather was fine, I applied myself to outdoor repair work on the RSPB cottage.

A source of dissatisfaction was lessening contact with the local, people. The crofters rarely came to the machair once the corn was sown, and, apart from regular visits to the Macdonalds at The Glebe or occasional conversations with Cameron at his gate, there seemed no opportunity to fraternise with the islanders.

It was gratifying when Lachie Fergusson from Balranald

township came to the caravan one morning and asked for himself and two of his friends to be taken to see the snowy owl. Lachie was interested in birds and it seemed a welcome sign of recognition that he should ask to be conducted to a bird which was more or less on hiw own land. Nor would it do the reserve's reputation any harm to be seen to receive Lachie, township clerk and church elder, a prominent and respect figure in the community.

It was like a church deputation. Lachie turned up at the prearranged time in his church-elder's black suit, plastic raincoat over one arm and best cloth cap in hand. While he came to the door, his friends, dressed in precisely the same way, stood by the noticeboard, scuffling their feet and looking boredly at the sky. We set off, walking in an absurd single file procession, up the track towards a point from which we'd have a good view of the bird.

I went first, jacketless and hatless in the warm morning sunshine, carrying binoculars, telescope and tripod. I played my warden's part, chattering about birds, stopping often to scan the marshes for anything which might interest the others. Lachie followed me and then the other two, all walking with hands behind their backs, raincoats held between elbow and hip, and with slow, even strides. It resembled an elder's Sabbath outing; but it wasn't Sunday, it was Tuesday, and in spite of the carried raincoats the sky was serenely cloudless.

Grey seal and pup

A party of birdwatchers coming on foot to the reserve stopped to stare, and were ignored. Lachie sometimes acknowledged my forced volubility with a polite 'Aye'; the other two were stolidly silent. I kept up my pointless chatter until we reached the viewpoint, erected the tripod, fastened the telescope to it and focused on the owl. The crofters in turn inspected the bird. It was a most accommodating owl, sitting most of every day in the same place on the wall above the marshes. Its life was easy, mainly sedentary, hunting a simple matter where there were many plump young rabbits. After brief excursions to kill and feed, the owl returned to the

Snowy owl

same spot where it slept, digested, and more than paid for its rabbits by displaying itself so clearly and consistently to scores of eager birdwatchers.

The sunlight was bright on the bird, the island air without trace of haze, and through the telescope every detail of plumage was visible. Yellow talons gripped the rock and whenever it opened them yellow owl eyes glared, completely belying an otherwise teddy-bearish appearance. On other occasions, such views had held birdwatchers riveted for hours.

Lachie squinted through the telescope for fully a minute. The other two took their turns, about the same length of time, then we stood by while Lachie made his pronouncement.

'It's very white,' he said. On that note of profundity I moved to dismantle the telescope when one of Lachie's friends showed a new interest in the view across the marsh.

'Just a minute, Lachie. Isn't that one of your cows, down there by the water?' I could see the beast, floundering around in the bog-bean, and instead of removing the telescope swung it round and re-focused it on the cow. Lachie shouldered me aside in his impatience to see the animal.

'Aye, it is, and dammit, she's stuck herself in the bog.'

The crofters forgot their English and jostled each other for views through the telescope. It was touch and go. She might sink or she might swim and Lachie was uncertain whether or not to dash off immediately for tractor and rope. Then with a squelch we could hear from the road, the cow heaved herself free and reached safety on the bank.

Ties were loosened, brows wiped with caps, raincoats discarded on the road. My visitors examined the telescope with new respect. With one of these, a crofter could spot a cow in trouble from his kitchen window. From the house he could see sheep far away on the hill. 'You could watch a cow drowning any time with one of those,' said one.

All the way back to the caravan we discussed optical equipment. I told them a little about the relative merits of different types. They were sharply interested now; we walked not in file but together, all eagerly talking. By the time we reached the caravan they had all resolved to buy not telescopes – they were too cumbersome – but strong standard binoculars.

Lachie thanked me effusively. An invitation to share an evening meal with him and his family was accepted. 'You can tell me more about binoculars,' he said. He had already forgotten the owl – but how well it would look in my end of season reports if I wrote that all the crofters had acquired binoculars and telescopes. No need to mention that they used them only for watching cows.

August is the holiday month: the time of children free from school, busy seaside resort beaches. The time of soft fruits becoming squashily overripe, wasps, flies; lethargic days with temperatures approaching the eighties and airless, sleepless nights.

Summer at Balranald seemed to come to its end in early August. The bird breeding season was over, the marshes and machairs were quiet except for corncrakes grating in the ripening corn. The flush of riotous colour in the machair flowers was already dying to autumn-tawny. It had been a poor, wet summer for the crofters' haymaking and now they had given up attempts to mow the grasslands or even to bring in what they had cut. Swathes and wind-dispersed hay coils lay blackening in autumnal mists, and the crofters turned to tinkering with machinery preparing for corn harvest.

I had been getting my own harvest safely in, taking stock of the bird breeding season on the reserve. Common waders had done very well. Of the rarer birds – the species for which Balranald is particularly noted – terns had only had an average year, with more pairs than usual attempting to breed but a lower proportion of young successfully fledged. One colony had been entirely wiped out when the belt of corn which the terns were using was sprayed with weedkiller. It had astounded me; a tractor-driven spray, sweeping up and down the rows, air acrid with the smell of it, progressive agriculture at last come to the machair. The terns had gone with the charlock; thereafter the field had grown a glorious crop of corn marigolds which completely choked the corn.

Corncrakes appeared to be holding their own, even increasing. They nested in the rough pastures and the marsh edges, then moved their young to the safety of cornfields which might not be cleared until mid-September. There was a pair of corncrakes in the cemetery at Goular, another pair in the nettle patch behind the cottage. The road skirting the marshes was a boundary between corncrakes' nesting territories in the fields on one side and marsh fringe iris beds on the other. Corncrakes gave Goular and Hougharry a noisy night life and Patricia guarded two pairs in the small area of Balranald House garden.

I became blasé about corncrakes, ceased to notice their calling. Visitors to the reserve drew my attention to them and were astonished when their intense interest wasn't shared. To me, they were almost domestic, little brown pullets which so often led their chicks in file past my window, whose crowing not only announced my morning but were a background cacophony to every night.

A pair of birdwatchers brought a tape recording of a corncrake's call and played it from their car. Instantly the place was alive with corncrakes. They gathered from iris bed, rush clump, sedge tussock and hayfield, intent on dismissing this intruder. They patrolled the road beside the car; they jumped onto the bonnet and stood barking in angry perplexity. They ignored the birdwatchers as they took photographs, generally satiating themselves with a bird which was always elusive, according to bird books, and threatened by extinction in Britain.

Had I realised how precarious these populations of corncrakes in

Uist in fact were, more attention might have been devoted to them. Unprecedented changes in agricultural methods now threaten to reduce the corncrakes in the islands as elsewhere, and mine may have been one of the last summers of their abundance.

More of my time was given to phalaropes in the hope that they might succeed and after years of absence reinstate themselves as one of Balranald's regular breeding birds. But neither of the nests on the reserve had produced any young. I had patiently sat among Hougharry township's malodorous rubbish at the edge of the loch, day after day, but hadn't seen a phalarope there since the end of June; only gulls, the inevitable lapwings and a mute swan which methodically produced six cygnets from its nest in the bank. Where my female phalarope was first seen the shallows were now dried, caked mud, spotted with swans' droppings and littered with whisky bottles and beer cans.

At Loch nam Feithean the male phalarope was too much in evidence. When it should have been sitting on eggs or tending young, it was flirting like a leisured dandy with the marshside dunlins. Then it moved to some lagoons where it gave pleasure to me and a few fortunate birdwatchers. In July it disappeared, having failed to produce any of the young which might have helped to maintain the Balranald population.

Red-necked phalarope (male)

It may have been one of the two reserve phalaropes which ended that summer for me so decisively, one evening during the first week of August. Most of my day had been spent mixing mortar for the cottage and, in apprentice fashion, blocking up cracks in the outside walls. It had been a hot, fly-ridden day, I had been interrupted frequently by visitors, and by late afternoon had had enough. I sluiced off mortar and sweat, then rather than rest at the caravan where more visitors would probably call before evening, I took a book, a flask of tea and a banana for a recreational dawdle to Traigh Iar.

At the beach there was a breath of onshore wind and fewer flies, and I lolled on the sward above the sands, trying my hardest not to be a nature reserve warden. People passed but I ignored them, opening my book, displaying the flask, behaving like any holidaymaker enjoying the beach. Habit, however, took over. Binoculars were raised to a crèche of mixed shelducks and eiders, swimming at the base of the headland, searching through seaweeds for small crabs which they flourished and beat against the rocks before swallowing them whole.

The ducks took fright, eiders diving and shelducks scrambling for higher rocks. A swirl like a small whirlpool broke to the head of a bull grey seal, nosing round the headland, pushing into shallow water on the heels of the departing ducks. It slid underwater and its dark bulk was netted by wave-shadow on white sands; then it surfaced with a large eel threshing in its jaws: a conger, 3ft long, as

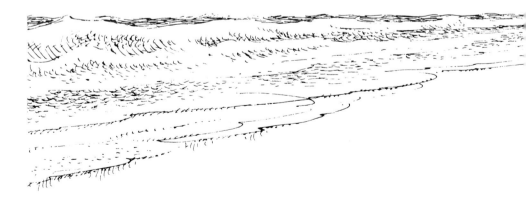

thick as a man's calf and extremely lively. The eel seemed boneless elastic, but the seal kept its grip. With a crunch that was audible on the beach, it bit through leg-thick sinew and bone and the eel dropped in two halves back into the water. The seal dived again, picked up the head half and surfaced, chewing. The innocuous round head of a seal bobbing offshore rather conceals tusk-sized teeth set in immensely powerful jaws. The seal finished the head half of the eel and, without so much as a burp, dived in search of the tail.

A couple of holidaymakers approached, beach strollers from a caravan parked in the dunes, exercising a small obstreperous dog. They stopped and he took a photograph of she standing like a heron on a boulder, silhouetted against the evening light on the sea. A Western Isles idyll. That photograph must have shown a dark blob flawing the sea's surface less than 20yd from the posing woman – the bull seal devouring the second half of its conger.

The couple's dog ran along the tideline, flushing a flock of sanderlings and I prepared myself for reassumption of my warden's role. They'd have to keep their dog under control before it cleared Traigh Iar of tired early autumn migrants. But one of the sanderlings was not a sanderling. It was slighter, darker, sharper winged, and it separated from the mist-like coherence of the main flock to arrow down alone to a sand pool. It didn't land like a typical wader on the shore of the pool but hit the water with a tiny splash and sat there, pertly spinning. A phalarope, again displaying that uncanny

ability to appear from nowhere and sit at one's feet.

If it was my male phalarope from Loch nam Feithean, it might be recognisable. After all, that bird was watched daily for weeks, long enough to enable me to detect individual colouring and mannerisms. I moved nearer the pool and sat down again. The holidaymakers had moved away, taking their dog with them. The phalarope did a quick circuit of the pool, then sat in the middle, pecking lightly at its rippled reflection. I refocused my binoculars on the bird and was just achieving a clear image when a footstep sounded on the sand behind me, a hand touched my shoulder.

'Excuse me, are you the bird reserve warden?'

Already that day that polite enquiry had been made more than a dozen times. Then it was freshly mixed mortar drying before application, now it was a restive phalarope. I could not then be otherwise engaged, or now be impatient with the attractive young woman whose hand had so lightly distracted me from my bird.

'Sit down. Look at that pool. There's a phalarope on it.' The woman sat as if stricken and we both raised our binoculars, but the pool's still surface mirrored nothing but a barnacle-studded rock.

Knot

The phalarope had gone, fused into the blue and silver and deepening gold of the island evening.

We gazed at the empty pool for a minute or two, me with despairing nostalgia, the woman as if this pool demanded special reverence. I pointed out the sanderlings, settled and feeding again at the wave's edge, and the crab-hunting sea ducks. I told her about the seal and the conger. She showed a polite interest, but it didn't compensate. When I left the beach half an hour later and glanced back, she was sitting motionless, binoculars trained on the empty sea pools.

Now the birds around the caravan were not corn buntings and twites singing their dry breeding season songs, but black-headed gulls come up from the marsh and beach to hunt for beetles among rampant nettles and dying umbelliferae around the ruinous walls of Goular township. Cameron came out with his scythe, apparently intending to cut some of the herbage down. When he saw me outside the cottage he thought better of working and came over for a chat, and to beg a cigarette. He and his dog between them attracted more flies than a croft-house midden, and I normally avoided long conversations, but this time a freshly mixed batch of mortar couldn't be left and I worked on while he talked.

After a short while it dawned on me that this was not Cameron's usual casual visit. He wanted more than to pass an hour of the interminable day with a cigarette. Today his requirements were more definite. He smiled, made an attempt at pleasantry, admiring my work, discussing the weather, sympathising with my loss of privacy to so many holidaymakers. Several times he moved to leave but turned back, as if trying to overcome reluctance to make some special request. At last he came out with it. He was troubled he said, by wallpapers.

'Peeling are they? I suppose it's the damp.'

No, it wasn't the wallpaper on the walls which worried him, it was the paper intended for the walls. He had ordered a catalogue of wallpaper patterns from a mail order firm and it had arrived by post that morning. He now had to select his paper and order it through the firm's agent in North Uist, Mary Macdonald, at The Glebe.

'Sounds simple enough.' I tried to be brisk, dismiss his worried look. It wasn't simple, though, for Cameron. He couldn't understand how to estimate quantity, or select the paper, or go about ordering the stuff. Above all, he didn't want Mary Macdonald to know how helpless he was. He didn't want her in his house in its present squalid condition and he didn't want to admit having grown so incapable as to require a woman's help. To appeal to Mary for help in overcoming a simple domestic problem: it was the beginning of becoming helpless as the senile are helpless, reliant as children on mothering women. Better to appeal to the stranger, since masculine interdependence is a perpetual feature of a landworking community.

We went over to Cameron's house and seated ourselves to each side of the catalogue which already stood open on the kitchen table. Cameron put a kettle on the gas ring. The house was relatively clean; sugar, milk and two cups stood ready. Cameron had evidently been preparing both himself and his house for this session.

The catalogue was almost a foot thick and a flick through it turned your mind into a kaleidoscope. He wanted a washable paper, which eliminated more than half the patterns.

'What about this? No, too garish. You don't want an intricate pattern, or you'll have trouble putting it up.' Cameron agreed with everything. Appealing to him for a final decision was confusing and quite irrelevant. He didn't want advice, he wanted me to choose. I selected a simple paper in innocuous pale brown.

'That's very nice,' said Cameron. 'That's chust what I had in mind.'

First operation over, we took a tea-break. Through the window we watched tourists milling around my caravan. It was satisfying to be in here with Cameron. We were natives of Goular, as distinct from the summer strangers outside. Cameron had no idea how to calculate the amount of paper he required. This was no deficiency of intelligence, simply that he was unaware that wallpaper arrived in rolls and had to be calculated in strips.

Ordering too, was a problem for him. His eyes were weak, he had difficulty in reading anything and not only was the layout of the form unfamiliar, but it was also written in a foreign language. The whole business of mail ordering was alien to him, whose only buying experience for years had been simple groceries from the mobile shop.

We proceeded to the matter of paint. Here Cameron was much more decisive. The only possible colours were the primaries and he wanted blue for the ceilings, red for the walls, and would I be sure to order a lot. If there was any left over when the inside of the house was finished, he'd paint the gate and the door of the byre, and maybe if there was an awful lot left, he'd do a bit to the outside walls of the house. I ordered several gallons each of red and blue and prayed that he'd run out of it before reaching the seaward-facing outside gable. Scarlet and cobalt in a Hebridean sunset would be altogether too much.

I travelled up with the order form to Mary and, a little more than a week later, delivered paper, paint and brushes to Cameron's door. Cameron took the materials inside and thereafter for a fortnight the door was closed, there was neither sight nor sound of Cameron. Iain passed very early one morning on his way to shoot rabbits on the machair and he reported seeing a very colourful Cameron at the back of the house, emptying a tin of something on the grass. So the old man was alive. But I didn't see him until one day he came to the caravan door, red and blue from cap to the soles of his slippers but elated, victorious.

The decoration was finished and I must come and see the house. Nothing had been attempted outside, which was a relief, but the interior was horrible. Paper had been stuck on anyhow, leaving gaps between the strips and between wall, floor and ceiling. A ragged hole had been torn to admit a bracket for a gas light. The paper was no longer a discreet off-brown; it was streaked with blue which had run down from the ceiling, and there were red and blue handprints all over it, as though a painted Cameron had been climbing the walls.

To ceilings Cameron had applied blue paint as thick as rendering. He had covered the required surface, but it showed deep brush marks, and strings and gobbets hung down like stalactites. Where blue ceiling met red wall there was an intermediate zone of purple, and dribbles of blue ran down the red walls in places almost to the floor. Everywhere, on shelves, table, floor and Cameron, were pools and patches of red, blue and various purples.

It was a nightmare but I didn't say so to Cameron. Nor to Mary when she asked me how the decorating had gone. I respected the old man's suspicion of well-intentioned women enough simply to mutter: 'Oh, not so bad. He's done a pretty thorough job.'

My own house improvements progressed quite rapidly once free of ornithological field-work and I was able to devote more time to

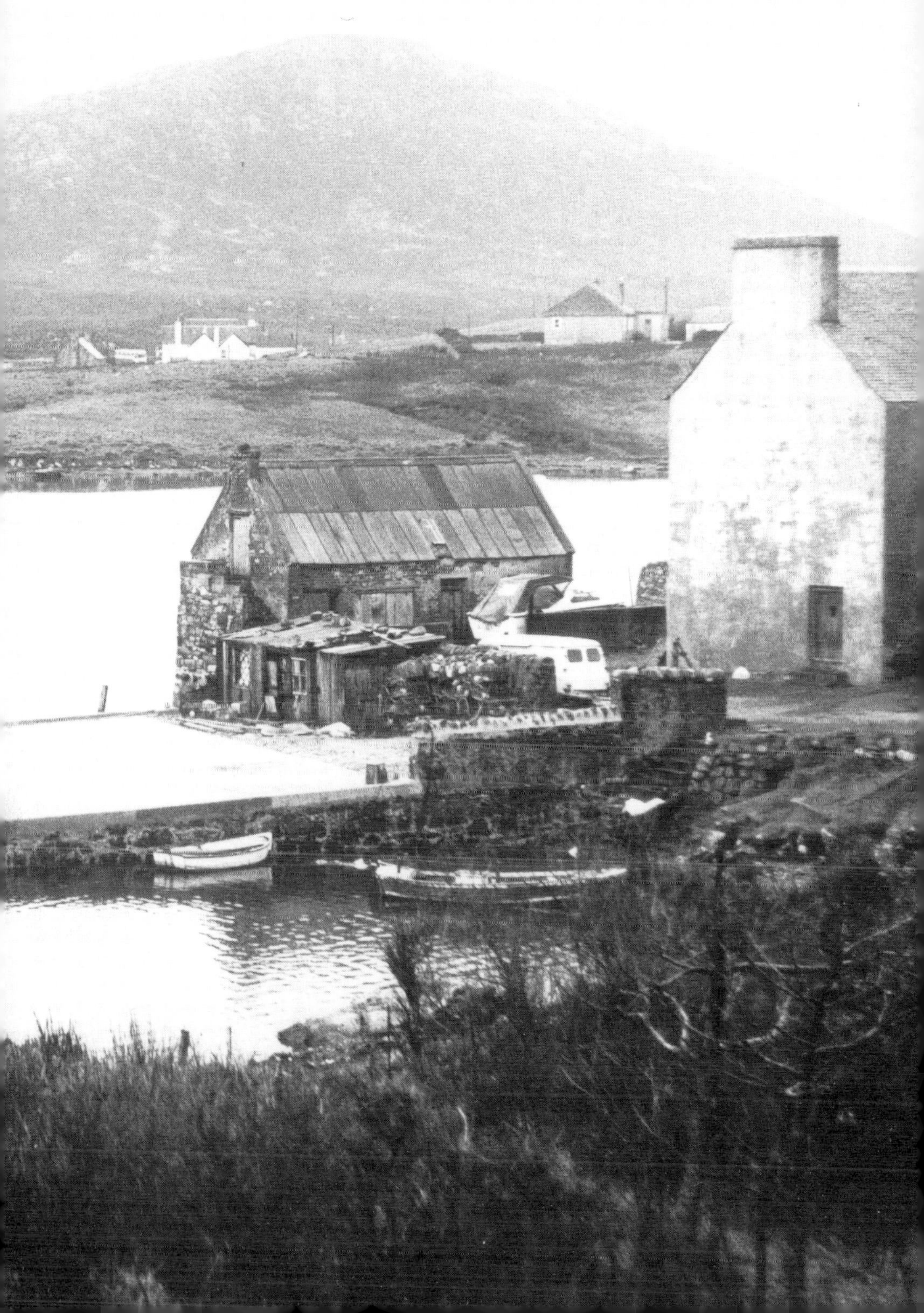

Seaflower at Lochmaddy pier

rendering, painting, amateur stonemasing and indoor carpentry. I didn't abandon birds altogether, but took walks in the early morning while the marshes were undisturbed and worked on the cottage through the middle part of the day – a simple routine which provided a fair balance of the practical and observational, solitude and company.

Deficiencies in the RSPB's supply of tools and materials were redressed more easily than anticipated. One could buy almost anything in the way of non-specialist hardware in the Uists simply by shopping around. I drove an 80-mile return journey to a crofter's store in South Uist for cement and Snowcem; purchased gravel cheaply from a quarry on the same island and found a timber merchant in an erstwhile Roman Catholic chapel in Benbecula. There was an adequate supply of small hardware to be had from a shop in North Uist. Reaching it entailed 8 miles of increasingly lonely dead-end road by the shore. The shop didn't advertise itself at all. Inside was an efficient little office and well-stocked orderly shelves; from outside it looked like an abandoned warehouse.

There were unsuspected repositories of other supplies. Despairing of ever obtaining good vegetables and fruit while in the islands, I found both available from the abattoir at Lochmaddy. Sacks of sound carrots and crates of apples, stacked under benches where thick-fisted butchers axed up carcases of deer and cows. Fresh bread was obtainable with other delicacies from the army's NAAFI in Benbecula. If I cared to make a 50-mile trip for it, even a wholemeal brown loaf. Among truly unavailable items were pipe-cleaners, fountain-pen ink and foolscap writing paper. But these were luxuries. I temporised with gulls' feathers, pencils and wrote memos to HQ on unlined vellum, as if they were letters to a treasured friend.

Rendering of the cottage was finished, new windows fitted, doors repaired and a spell of fine weather enabled me to slap three coats of Snowcem on the outside walls in a single week. The cottage had been inconspicuous, one of a huddle of grey-walled ruins. Now for more than a mile across the machair I could admire my little white home in the west.

Happy, noisy and dusty hours passed without my noticing them while shelves were made for the warden's room, screens, more shelves and boards for displays in the reception area. As a final exercise in handymanship, an inclining pigeon-hole cupboard was put together for future wardens' documents. It was spindly and shaky and I forgot to sandpaper it, but screwed it to the wall and it sufficed.

After some display design and final paperwork, the Balranald season could be brought to a satisfactory close. The weather was fine; indoor sedentary habits had long been discarded. Besides, I had been working hard and continuously and needed a break. At the first chatter of cutter and binder on the machair, I went to help the crofters with their corn harvest.

Oats and rye. A little barley. Poppies and bugloss, charlock, forget-me-not, corn marigold. A nutritious bundle of machair summer, every sheaf. Murdo drove the tractor, Mary sat on a metal seat high on the binder, operating a lever which regulated the height of the cutting bar above the uneven ground. Iain and I stacked sheaves. Cutting started at around ten in the mornings, by which time routine jobs at the house were done and dew had dried off the corn.

Everyone started at the same time. At 9 o'clock the machair was quiet except for golden plovers calling as they fed in flocks on the new stubble. Skylarks roosted where they had once had nests, under furrows and tussocks. They no longer sang but in the early morning flew under my feet with frightened chirps. An hour later the machair was a scene of rural industry. From each township a score of binders were out and working, clattering up and down the unfenced strips, wheels with wooden guiding bars rhythmically turning, and the stubble now littered with bound sheaves.

The stackers would be out: wives, mothers, children taking unofficial leave from school, relatives home for a working holiday, straightening what had fallen during the night of yesterday's sheaves before starting on today's. People grouped at this stage of the morning, newsing to be done before the rhythm of the day's work separated and silenced. Chatter of the cutting blades, engines of tractors. A haze of blue diesel smoke to replace mists of morning. Men already stripping to shirt-sleeves and women wiping palms on kitchen aprons. Only the children worked at their hardest now. They would have this brief period of diligence before becoming bored with stacking. Dogs on the loose made a renegade pack and headed for rabbit warrens in the sand-dunes.

A busy, noisy, social scene. Gladly abandoning solitary beach walking, I simply wandered over to the Macdonalds' strip and started stacking. Iain worked at the other end of the field; some time before midday we would meet and wish each other good morning.

The work didn't always go smoothly. Cutters and binders are ancient machines, of traditional style except drawn by tractors rather than horses or oxen. Many of the binders are kept outside, rarely overhauled, expected to work at the beginning of each harvest after a merest smearing of grease. Metal parts rust, wooden parts rot in the winters and there are many breakdowns at the start of every harvest. Spare parts for these obsolete machines are difficult to get and they are held together by improvisation; a nail here, a twist of wire or string there, enough to enable the machine to survive just one more season. So often that it ceases to be of any interest to a mere stacker, the tractor and binder combination stops and the rhythm of work is broken for repairs.

The commonest faults were failures in the binding mechanism. This is a fairly intricate piece of machinery which binds the cut corn into a sheaf, tightens string around the waist of the sheaf, ties a knot and cuts the string. Sometimes the knife would fail and the sheaves come out bound together; a string of sheaves scores of yards in length, which it might take an hour to disentangle.

Very often the binding mechanism would fail completely and the cut corn spray out erratically over the stubble. Then we had to bind by hand. Iain was competent at this but Mary was expert, having harvested as a girl before the days of twine and mechanical binding. She tried to teach me the art of hand binding. A double handful of corn, lightly grasped, stalk end foremost. Settle the loose sheaf on the hip. (I was at a disadvantage here – Mary's hips were considerably wider than mine.) Without looking, run your right palm over the head of the sheaf, stroke the down-bent ears of corn, select a few strands of the longest and jerk them free. This is your cornstalk string. In one movement enwrap the loose sheaf, make an encircling cornstalk waist and tighten. So far all is touch and rhythm, but the final knot is a brutal process, a finger-tearing wrench that jerks the waist of the sheaf narrow, splits and crushes the lissom stalks.

My fingers were too short or the stalks too long and the unbound sheaf cascaded over my knee to the ground. Propped with three of its kind, my sheaf would collapse, the other sheaves in the stook with it.

The flails broke, the blades struck stones and had to be sharpened. There were too many of 'then plutty flowersh' among the corn, making the sheaves unmanageable, threatening to prevent the stacked sheaves from quickly drying. Iain and I stood around, waiting for the cutting to begin again, at first grateful for the rest and then bored. Iain suggested a sortie into the dunes with the shotgun but Murdo, sensing a slackening of attention, dropped his hammer and grabbed the scythe. The scythe was always carried on the tractor for cutting marshy edges or rough, stony places. Now Murdo swung it in a wide swathe down his strip. He was not a large man, Murdo, nor a young one; but he kept Iain and me sweating after him, binding his sheaves for the rest of the morning; and while we rested at midday he repaired the cutters for work during the afternoon.

Mary often had other commitments and then Iain took her place on the binder while I stacked sheaves alone. She left the field an hour before midday and went to The Glebe; and then we would all work with an eye on the house, waiting for her to reappear with the midday food. Some crofters drove home for lunch, their wives having gone before them to boil the inevitable potatoes. But Mary brought a basket from the house and we ate ours in the open field.

I enjoyed those harvest-day lunches. If Mary had been absent all morning the scones and oatcakes might still be warm from a fresh baking. Butter melted in the sun, cheese and chocolate softened, the strong scalding tea was surprisingly refreshing. The best of the break came after the food, when Mary packed the remains into the basket and we leaned back replete for half an hour's drowse. No one slept, but all looked through half-closed eyes across stubble and marsh to the township.

Houses vague in the midday haze, hills behind lost in the general blueness, even the loch looked hot, flat and pale like sun-beaten metal. It was contemplation without thought. There was no urgency to find a subject for talk, but if a figure showed among the houses we decided who it was, then idly discussed where the person had been and was going, why he or she should be out during the midday hour. A strange car on the road was subject for similar

Stacks of corn on the machair
(inset left) Stacking corn; (right) An old-fashioned threshing machine

curiosity, idle and gentle, a natural awareness of people and event, most sensitively attuned to one's own township but extending to include in less detail the whole island.

A glance over the strips to compare our morning's work with others': envy of Robertson whose two sons had come home to help, sympathy for Macallister whose tractor had broken down. Some inter-family rivalry; if he thought he was behind, Murdo would have us up and working again before we had rested our full hour.

Afternoon was hot and golden. As the sun moved from directly overhead into the western sky, so the air seemed to fill with flakes of golden light, more iridescent than the corn, less substantial even than pollen. It may have been hallucination, my mind overfull with the colour of ripe corn, for no one else seemed to experience this drift of intangible chaff, but it hovered around me every harvest afternoon.

The children tired first. They played about for a while until they irritated their parents, then soon after lunch they straggled away towards home. Older people who had been stacking sheaves steadily for five or six hours began to feel a weariness of the legs by mid-afternoon. They gathered and sat in the shade below a parked trailer, watching sons and daughters possessively, but in a social group of their own.

My feet felt hot, the sandy soil and stubble seemed to burn them through rubber boot soles. The stalks and sharp ears of corn pricked my forearms to rawness and my fingers blistered with lifting sheaves by their strings. Some perverse pride kept me going for four hours from lunch to tea-break. Never has lukewarm tea from a flask seemed more resuscitating; it hit my parched throat with a bite like spirit and after a gulp or two I could even swallow another of Mary's oatcakes. I might have carried on, working with Murdo and Iain into the evening, but Mary departed and I took the opportunity to leave, before the length and repetitiveness of the work made it into a test of endurance rather than a pleasure.

Helping with the harvest in Uist was an experience of physical involvement with a rural tradition not obsolete in Britain. In remote areas of the Highlands and elsewhere among the islands, there are crofters who still cut their corn pockets among the rocks with scythes and sickles; but in Uist the harvest, with one or two annu-

196

ally recurring tasks, was a communal affair. There was no ceremony of harvest beginning, no feast in the byre when the last sheaves were gathered, but the sense of community was there.

It was something felt through hearing those old binders at work everywhere on the machair; in the patchwork scene of corn strip, fallow strip, stubble with sheaves casting lengthening shadows, black on bronze. It was there in the lunch-time gossip and half-asleep surveillance, and the old people drawing together away from the young. I was involved with the community effort for eight hours a day during a week of their harvest and appreciative of the experience. But eight hours a day was enough.

So as the tractor started up again after tea I wandered away from the workers, up over the machair and through the sand-dunes to one of the western beaches. When I dropped down the face of the sand-dunes onto the sands, the harvest was quite cut off from me, out of sight and hearing. My place was now with the hard white level strand, where there were no people, only waders flying and feeding along the edges of the sea. Pleased for the moment not be a crofter, or anyone but me, here, alone at the land's limit, I sauntered easily over the sand.

If the tide was out I went far over banks of rotting seaweed to sand and rock pools along the lowest littoral. A between-world, neither land nor sea, where stumps of kelps stuck up through drifts of sand like a stunted tideline forest, and life in the pools carried on its strange rhythm of exposure to air, immersion by sea-water. Waders ran from pools to rocks to sands, in and out of the lapsing waves, stitching land and sea together.

Sanderlings, crisp little bits of foam themselves, chased the waves. Gulls slid about the sky over headlands where they had nested in spring. Every evening for a hot week I stripped off clothes and laid them on a rock above the tide's reach, then slipped into the cold sea for a swim. The Uist sea was always cold, always just too glassily clear and clean to be entirely comfortable. After a short while I came out to run myself warm along the sand; sat naked on the rock near my clothes while a breeze dried the water on my skin and left a light crust of salt. Then I rose and dressed and walked away with the half-moon shape of my swim-wet buttocks still drying on the rock.

Winter stacks of corn at Hastin

Up the dune face and very tired now, feet dragging in soft sand. Through dunes alive with rabbits, by damp interdune slacks where the only flowers were autumn gentians past their best and ragwort at its sturdiest. Yellow of ragwort merged with shadows between dunes. No workers now, everyone gone home, the place mine as with sunset behind me I came over the machair, brushing through waist-high standing corn or threading sheaves standing on stubble. The corn was already damp, there was a mist over the marshes, thickening above loch and creek where fully grown duck families were out, dabbling and quacking.

The moon would be rising soon, harvest sickle cutting a blue field above Eaval; another harvest day over and weather set fair for tomorrow. But golden plovers were restless, flighting from beach and marsh to feed in the stubbles, and in their calls was winter rain.

Iain's main spare-time interest was shooting. He was a member of North Uist's clay pigeon shooting club and with them in their inter-island contests won many prizes for individual performance. This was almost the whole of his leisure life; he might travel with the team to another island and be away for a day; otherwise he rarely left home, or took part in any activity which might separate him from his family and township. When the girls gathered at The Glebe ostensibly to visit Mary, actually to display themselves to this most eligible young crofter, Iain simply removed himself, not like so many of his contemporaries to a round of hotel bars and roadside drinking places, but down to the machair with spaniel and shotgun.

We walked out one morning together to begin harvesting one of The Glebe strips close to the marshes. As we approached, a score of mallard flew from the edge of the corn, circled, and slanted to land in shallow water in the marsh. They were in dull moulting plumage, but a splendid sight all the same, straining up in panic, banking with sunlight on their wings, gathering to a tight flock, in unity of impulse arrowing down and landing with a series of splashes.

Iain had an eye for them. His body lifted as the birds rose. He was raising an imaginary gun. As they turned to sweep in he pulled a mental trigger and at least one duck came crippling down. Sportsman's instinct. Also the ducks would be eating the corn; very soon they would move up over the stubble to feed on fallen grain and stacked sheaves. Ducks could climb on to the sheaves, flattening the stooks and soiling them with their droppings; and not only ducks, but greylag geese which bred on the moors and as soon as their young could fly, travelled in family parties to machair, salt-marsh and fresh-marsh.

Geese, so much larger and heavier than ducks, Iain considered a real menace. The weather might be bad and the sheaves stand un-gatherable for weeks. Every night the wildfowl would flatten more stooks and eat and leave copious droppings, so that in the end much of the harvest would be soiled or rain-rotted, hardly worth the trouble of taking in.

I was sceptical. Curlews, lapwings, golden plovers and crows gathered in vast flocks to feed on sheaves and stubble. Small birds were even more numerous: starlings, sparrows, corn buntings, twites and skylarks; clouds of them every evening, uncountable as locusts in a swarm or blackfly on a crop of beans. Then there were rabbits, rats, mice, voles, and in some areas unfenced sheep and cattle wandered across the harvest fields, tearing at the sheaves. Wildfowl were only a small part of the life which concentrated on the machair to share in the crofters' harvest. How did Iain propose to deal with the skylarks, or the rats; or even the rain which is the greatest threat of all to any island harvest?

All day, whenever the tractor stopped, we could hear the ducks splashing around in the marsh. An increasing tension affected Iain, like a wire drawing him away from the sheaves towards an image of himself by an evening creek, spaniel at his feet, shotgun under his arm. At lunch-time we could see splashes from the ducks, little spouts of water jumping higher than the waterside rushes. 'There's teal in there, as well,' gritted Iain, forgetting to eat his chocolate. Teal, fastest and most enticing of wildfowl, also tastiest on the plate. In the afternoon a dozen geese, two adults and ten fully grown, this year's goslings, came down to the loch. They sat, complacently preening, in full view.

'They'll be among the sheaves tonight.' Iain suffered a distracted remainder of the working day; he kept stopping with a sheaf dangling from each hand, staring over the marshes. He was calculating which line the birds would take from water to corn. Would they walk or fly, and if they flew, under which sheaf or tussock should he lie, to make full use of shadow and light from the late-rising waxing moon?

Lapwing and sheep

It was early in the year for wildfowling, migrants and the wintering birds were not yet arriving. The season for orthodox wildfowling sportsmen had hardly begun, but an island crofter has an earlier season. Not only is he permitted to shoot duck and geese out of season in defence of his corn, but he lives with wildfowl which breed numerously on his land. He knows when the birds are flighting and recognises the possibility of one for the pot, and no official close season will stop him responding to the impulse to have a night on the marsh.

Of my reaction to his wildfowling, Iain wasn't sure, and it troubled him. Would I, as a warden, object? I had no authority to interfere with what was perfectly legal sport, but would it cause offence to me personally, spoil an otherwise friendly relationship? It was best to be direct, so before leaving the harvest field that night I appealed to Iain not, please, to shoot the Loch nam Feithean marshes. The snowy owl was still there and I would rather it stayed until it chose to go. Anyway, I would be at Balranald for only a few more weeks and it would please me to retain memories of it as a sanctuary. A few more weeks wasn't much to ask; meanwhile, couldn't he shoot one of the lochs outside the reserve?

Iain was surprised by my direct approach. He hadn't realised how obvious he had made his intention to go shooting. But he recovered himself quickly and gave me a grin which was part friendly mockery.

'It's all right about your precious marshes. I don't want to shoot there anyway. Much more chance of a goose on Vausary and I might get a rabbit on the way. I'll be starting out about seven tonight. Are you coming?'

It was my turn to be surprised but, though hesitant, didn't show it. Why shouldn't I have an evening's wildfowling?

Loch Vausary lay about 3 miles north of The Glebe, close to the coast which here is mainly rocky. It is a machair loch like Loch nam Feithean, but its former marshlands had long ago been drained and it had none of Loch nam Feithean's indented shape or rushy margin. The most interesting thing about Vausary was that it demonstrated the fate of machair marshes once crofters had conceived the idea of draining them. Its dry rocky banks lacked variety, its surface unbroken by vegetative growth seemed sterile, scenically unattractive and relatively poor wildlife habitat.

Vausary and its shores held fewer waders and dabbling duck than Balranald's wetlands, but its deeper water did attract diving duck, and the grassy slopes above the loch provided grazing for geese, especially when richer machair areas were disturbed by crofting activity, such as harvesting. It would be a lifeless spot in winter, but it would have a good goose population now, in early September.

The geese, Iain explained, would feed on the grass while there was still summer nutrient in it, and roost for safety in the centre of the loch. In October or November, whenever harvesting was finished and the machair undisturbed, the flocks would disperse to marshes like Balranald's, and the tidal inlets with salt-marsh like Loch Paible, from which they could feed out onto the after-harvest stubbles.

We left The Glebe just before seven, while there was still enough light to see rabbits on our walk across machair and sand-dunes to Vausary. I didn't want to shoot, never having handled more than a child's popgun in my life, and not wanting to begin now; but Iain insisted that I carry his .22 rifle, while he shouldered a shotgun.

There were rabbits aplenty in the croftlands as we skirted

Hougharry, but Iain respected the unwritten prerogative of others to quarry on their own land. He restrained his sporting instincts until we had climbed a high fence and reached the common land of corn strips and dunes further north. To our left lay the grassy turf which stretched down to the headlands and the washing noise of a quiet sea among rocks. To our right were smooth marram-crested dunes, some entirely grassy, some with sandy slopes or deep sand-filled craters.

A rabbit paradise. They could make endless warrens in the dunes, and come out to feed and gambol on the short turf, out to the extreme tips of the headlands. They could organise rabbit sports on inter-dune areas and level as playing fields; they could choose whether to eat sweet salad of clover and daisies or nibble the savories of sea pinks, plantains and thyme. They could parliament on the headlands, rest from feeding and breeding to discuss rabbit affairs or invent rabbit legends, while the sea whispered below them and the moon laid a path from their headland to the even more ideal rabbit grounds of grassy off-shore islands.

Rabbits are everybody's prey: there were crow-picked, weather-bleached skeletons everywhere in the sand. A buzzard lifted from a dune and a family of ravens circled a headland. There were dog scratchings and otter prints in the harder sands, and half-feral township cats lived and bred in old warrens. Later in the month all scavengers would feast on victims of myxomatosis; meanwhile rabbits were snarable and shootable and in less than a quarter of an hour Iain had killed four. He shot them sitting, hardly seeming to take time to aim, and he cleaned them expertly with a sharp knife before dropping them into a sack.

It looked so easy and there were so many rabbits. I thought of the cost of bacon, my only meat. Iain suggested a try with the .22. The rifle had a telescopic sight. I rested the rifle on a dune crest, took careful aim and shot my first rabbit cleanly through the head. From the same position, shot two more. The ridiculous animals didn't run away when one was killed; they sat on like targets at a seaside booth, and we strolled over and picked them up. There was no need for the spaniel, all were shot through the head, quite dead.

In five minutes, enough meat for a fortnight. A callous but clean business, functional rather than sporting. I liked the precision of the

.22, the killing with a minimum of noise and fuss, and decided that I had a talent for shooting with a rifle.

Now it was getting dusk and there must be no more shooting before Vausary. Iain had hoped to reach the loch before the geese came in to roost, but he miscalculated – excusably since this was his first outing of the season – and the geese were already on the loch when we arrived. We disturbed them, appearing over the skyline of dunes, and fifty or sixty greylags rose as a single flock, honking, threshing their wings wildly, rising very slowly in spite of all the noise and effort. They gained height, lost initial panic, and flew in a wide steady circle above the loch. Goose-droppings pattered down on shore and water. The flock drew itself into echelon, the honking quietened to the conversation geese make when purposefully travelling, and they beat steadily away and out of sight to the north.

The loch rocked itself to stillness. There was now no goose or duck on it. Iain showed no disappointment but led the way to the shore where goose-feathers and droppings littered the stony shallows. 'They might come back,' he said. 'If we hide ourselves and wait, we might get a shot at them yet.'

Greylag geese

From Vausary's shore there was a causeway of stones extending to a thin peninsula almost to the centre of the loch. Once it had been a route to an island 'dun' or ancient fort, but this had gone and now there was only a small grassy island at the causeway's end. We sat on this island, low, near the shore of the loch, so that our outlines would not be seen by an incoming bird.

The September night was calm, the water still at our feet. Yet the sea beyond the western headlands was creased by its own motions, and it made a continuous low murmuring along the coast. There is no absolute stillness by the sea. We could hear waders calling down there, among the tide-washed rocks, and gulls were still circling and squalling. We were hidden but not enclosed; there was all that shelterless flatness of sea to the west, giving a combined sense of exposure and freedom.

Iain shifted his feet and ripples went out towards the middle of the loch. An incautious movement, surely not typical of Iain when wildfowling. The ripples died away, then Iain shifted again and the barrels of his shotgun grated on stones. Something was wrong with him, some tension wouldn't allow him to be still. The smooth surface of the loch seemed to image the new feeling, as if it was drawing itself tight, like a sheet to the point of tearing.

'I have a thing to tell you,' said Iain. I waited. 'They won't like me telling you this and I wasn't meaning to. But I wass thinking about it and it doesn't seem right. It's that I've got to dig a drain into the marshes, from the sea to Loch nam Feithean. The township want it done and they are hiring a machine, and I've got to do it starting this winter.'

The words were like stones thrown into the loch, shattering a calm image of the island. I didn't answer before grasping the full significance of what Iain said. Then it wasn't a time for angry remonstrance; to argue with him was worse than pointless, it would have been made ridiculous by that setting, the mists forming over the loch, the sea darkening, the inevitability of night drawing in.

I asked for details, wanting to know the worst. It wasn't in fact a matter of digging a new drain, but cleaning a former channel which had become choked. Starting at the sea exit of the water from the entire marsh catchment, Iain and his mechanical shovel would first remove sand and shingle from the beach, then follow a canalised stream from loch to loch, until he reached Loch nam Feithean.

The last stretch of drainage was a direct cut into the body of the marshes. I knew this existing choked channel well, a ditch like a slim pond where the water lay clear and still around iris and marsh willow-herb, water forget-me-not and brooklime, where summer mats formed of lush watercress and bog-bean. This loveliness was crossable by a plank, my secret bridge from one bank of rush and marsh orchids to the other, paths through wind-quivered bog cotton during my springtime censusing rounds . . .

An ancient drainage system. But if Iain dug a deeper channel to the sea, the entire water table would be lowered. In my mind all the marshland flowers, waders, wildfowl, rushes, wetland sedges, insects and otters – all washed down the deep new channel and disappeared out to sea. No, surely, it was impossible.

The trouble, Iain explained, was the cattle. The beach-wandering, kelp-chewing, loveable machair cattle. Three townships had common grazing adjoining the marsh and the cattle needed access to marshland freshwater. Otherwise, the machair ranges were dry, nowhere for cattle to drink among cultivated strips, sand-dunes and beaches. The cattle were moved down from the hill pastures when harvest was over in late autumn, and all winter each township's herd ranged the full extent of its machair from marshes to sea.

Once the grazing was gone, the cattle were fed on corn harvested the previous autumn, and they augmented this by eating the thick kelps which winter storms brought to the beaches. All winter there was little conflict between cattle husbandry and wetland, as the cattle moved only into the edge of the marshes to drink, and there were often flood flashes in hollows in the open machair and between sand-dunes.

It was spring when the cattle were threatened by the marsh. Then they had to go further in to find open water, crossing deep channels, and places where the surface vegetation was like a crust over a bottomless bog. Not only were the cattle attracted by the water, but they found bog-bean stems and rushes succulently growing long before there was any new growth on machair grassland. The cattle preferred the green water plants to the corn on which they were fed, and by spring the corn was in shortest supply.

For food and drink, in April and May, the cattle floundered in the

Harvesting bladderwrack

marshes. They plunged through surface mosses and unstable mats of rush and sedge. Inevitably they fell into creeks, wallowed up to their necks in liquid peat and couldn't heave themselves out. Some cattle drowned – infuriating to the crofters who had fed them all the long winter, especially if the drowned animal was a cow due to calve that same spring. Other wallowing cattle were pulled out alive, by ropes or fishing-nets winched to tractors on the banks; very often a cow treated in this way suffered some fatal internal injury and heavily pregnant cows might abort their calves.

Iain's dichotomy was plain: sympathy for the preservation of the marsh, encouraged by friendly relations with the RSPB wardens, including myself, and his growing interest in wildlife; opposed by his loyalty to the community, his family, his township and the neighbouring townships. Iain knew that unlike most young crofters he questioned the township ethic and was already uncertain of his identity. But although he had misgivings, and would therefore suffer as he did it, he would act as the township demanded and take a mechanical shovel to the marsh.

It was almost dark. The geese wouldn't come back to Vausary

208

now. We shouldered our guns and rabbits and walked back to The Glebe, where I ate a cheerful evening meal with the Macdonalds. It had been good to see and hear those geese gather over the loch; a hint of winter in that spearhead of birds against clear sky, welcome after the cloying days of a hot August harvest. Before winter fully came it was time for migration. The waders would be moving south and in less than a month I, too, would be leaving.

Iain came with me to the door of The Glebe that night and I thanked him with equal emphasis for the night's sport and for telling me about the plans to drain the marshes. We wouldn't mention the draining again, and I determined to report Iain's information to the RSPB and then to forget it. Observation and recording was my role, nothing could be done to prevent this loss of the marshes; it was best not to admit any emotional attachment which might spoil enjoyment of these last weeks. All the way to the caravan from The Glebe, moonlight glittered on the bays and creeks of Loch nam Feithean. I tried to see only the beauty of the scene, none of the irony.

The crofters were having trouble with their cows; but Britain is everywhere losing its fens, woodlands, hedges, salt-marshes. Loch Vausary was prose – what price this pocket of wetland poetry at Balranald?

I didn't sleep much that night. Dawn found me with map spread on the caravan table and a mind teeming with night-spawned ideas. Loch nam Feithean curving round Goular cemetery. There was that vital drainage channel, a simple black line with an arrow pointing seawards. Only the arrow was misleading; there was no permanent outgoing flow.

Each side of the loch was indented into bays, and beside the bays were areas of undefined extent, covered by the reed tuft symbol de-

North Uist

noting marsh. These were the vital pockets where the water level fluctuated, creating soft patches with rushes when levels were low, shallow lagoons in time of flood: habitat for wetland flowers, nesting and feeding birds – and hazardous to cattle.

At the west end of Loch nam Feithean, the division between wet and dry land was ill defined. Here, the lagoons, creeks and bays of the loch were separated by narrow spits of terrain intermediate between land and water. Given a dry season they might be stands of rushes, in a wet year they would be under water. At any time they were unmappable and it would be suicidal for any land creature to walk there – cow, crofter or RSPB warden. This was the province of ducks, migrant waders, phalaropes; the heart of the marsh. West of it was a gradual petering out of the wetland, past one or two isolated meres, through the extensive belt of marsh which was flooded only in winter. Tall sedges and umbelliferous plants grew thickly here, before the land lifted almost imperceptibly clear of wetland and became fifty more yards of cultivable machair.

I drew a thoughtful pencil line across this western end of the marsh. All the open water was to the east of my line, only a narrow strip of marsh to the west of it. Suppose, just suppose, this line were a fence. All the cattle of the townships would be kept west of the fence, excluded from the drinking water of the marsh. But it was just possible, if holes were dug into the narrow marsh area west of the fence, that they might hold water which cattle could drink during any dry spell that occurred while they were kept on the machair. The holes would be shallow, their edges firm, and the cattle would never be in danger of drowning when they drank there.

I turned my attention to the east side of the imaginary fence, to the marshes, now free of any agricultural use. The possibilities seemed infinite and exciting. Managed for wildlife rather than as dubious pasture for grazing farmstock, the true potential of this area might be realised.

To some extent, grazing cattle kept the shallowest and narrowest waters free of encroaching vegetation. This would have to be compensated for, by cutting and digging. But if digging, why not the excavation of more pools, creation of even more open waters than were present before? It would be marvellous for the wildfowl and it wouldn't influence the cattle at all, behind their fence.

I had to sit back and rest. A thin drizzle was falling outside; it was a grey dawn through the windows but my eyes would see only ideals, visions of a transformed Balranald.

Wildfowl and waders are the birds of the marshes. Diving ducks need fairly deep water for feeding, dabbling ducks need shallow lagoons. Some wildfowl, like wigeon and geese, appreciate short grasses which they nibble like sheep. Most waders, migrants and residents, in winter and summer require vegetation-free silt or water shallow enough for wading and probing. Different species of wader require different depths of water, but none of them use deep water for feeding nor can they utilise areas where vegetation is long. The truly tangled areas of the marsh, the drier parts where sedges grew in huge tussocks and the hogweed plants stood tall and dense as an herbaceous plantation, were useful only to certain species of both waders and wildfowl for nesting and providing protective covering for their young.

All types of terrain were necessary, but the habitat in shortest supply, and the absence of which might already be a limitation on bird numbers, was the shallow water with waterweeds, where banks of silt and short vegetation were exposed in times of drought. The ideal feeding habitat could be created by shallow digging and it would supply dabbling ducks and waders, whether migrants, winter residents or birds which nested deep in the long vegetation of the drier areas.

My pencil was busy again. It created a series of lagoons, wavy edged and with islands within pools to give maximum cover for the birds and places where they could rest from feeding, could sleep and preen. There would be many pools, not all excavated in a single season but over many years so that some would have shallow water and some would have vegetation in various stages of colonisation.

It was a rotational system for farming a wildfowl crop which would be seen, but never gathered in: a waterfowl garden, a wetland utopia. My pencil stopped its doodling; I leaned back the better to enjoy this vision: a mosaic of lagoons where wildfowl splashed, quacked and dabbled among waterlilies and bog-bean flowers. Waders picked their way delicately between sleeping ducks on the banks and islands; others were song flighting over the sedges where ducklings scuttled and wader chicks ran. On the green rabbit-clipped mounds moved veritable herds of geese and wigeon, and diving ducks porpoised happily around the deeper waters of the loch. Within the fence and wetland cornucopia all was uninhibited noise and colour, while outside the fence birdwatchers and botanists rubbed shoulders with smiling uncontentious crofters and well-watered but dry-footed cattle.

Curlew

Before Iain had mentioned drainage my wardening season had been more or less over, bar the paperwork; now I became busier even than during the bird breeding time in the spring. Definite plans must be submitted to the RSPB for approval and then taken to the clerks of all three relevant townships. Field-work: the ground to be surveyed, the physical possibility of excavation assessed; paper-work: maps to be drawn, the vision made cogent by diagrams and written exposition; and public relations: people to be written to, seen, placated, wherever possible impressed. Three weeks at most to do it in. But a visionary enthusiasm like mine defies time limits and that same drizzly morning a start was made.

I waded off into the misty wet levels of the marsh carrying notebook, a tape measure and a spade. The drizzle stopped but the mist persisted, dragging through long, water-beaded vegetation as I chopped holes in the marsh, west to east. I took an 18in square from each hole and dug down to hard sand. It wasn't soil, any of it, only tangled fibre of unrotted peat-preserved sedge, grass and roots, a foot or more in depth over a base of clean white sand. The holes all started to fill with water immediately. They were plotted on my map and given numbers. In a day or two I would come and measure the depth of water in each, try to estimate how deep any hole would have to be dug to hold water all through a summer of average rainfall.

One thing was immediately established as soon as I pushed the spade into the ground at the first hole and levered up the section of turf. It would be hard work, here, digging holes. It required a sharp spade and a good deal of thrust to cut through that vegetation; not a bit like digging a tilth or buttery slabs of moorland peat. This Loch nam Feithean stuff was like a tangle of subterranean wire.

Some open water during wetter spells could be achieved by mowing glades in the vegetation, but the permanent lagoons would have to be excavated. It was beyond the capacity of one man; it would require volunteers, conservation enthusiasts, schoolchildren. Perhaps the army staff from their base in Benbecula could be persuaded to do something useful like this rather than waste time and money making bangs over the sea. A show of interest and industry like this would impress the crofters: a wildlife-rich wetland, something to be worked for, not just a passive idea.

The complex marsh edge was mapped, channels running into it from drier ground and other existing ground features. A whole history of land division was evident, from walls which once followed the boundaries of crofts to sheepfolds and what might at one time have been byres and houses. The marks of former habitation had long grown over, superseded by estate banks and ditches and disused shooting butts built on the sites of shielings. Finally, I plotted the existing boundaries, wire fences separating the commonlands of the townships.

By late in the afternoon the map showed most of the relevant topographical features of the marshes. All the little details of water and land distribution, vegetation type, hummocks and hollows, vital to a naturalist but absent from even the largest scale OS maps.

A separate map was drawn, fitting my intended lagoons and islands into the existing features, drawing in the fence which could make the whole thing possible and ensuring that the cattle had large holes from which to drink. Then, with the ground plan of my projected wetland propped against the breadbin for reference, I put all my ideas into writing.

215

It was necessary to approach the township clerks in person and explain my ideas verbally, referring to maps. A written exposition would not be unintelligible to the crofters who are as literate as most beaurocrats, more painstaking in their assimilation of written fact and on average at least as intelligent. But crofters would be deterred by the formality of a written document; it would seem like some threat from an officialdom of which they were inherently suspicious. Some high-sounding ecological jargon would inevitably be contained in a written account and at the first hint of it the crofters would turn the whole idea down. To persuade the crofters I must rely on their sympathy for me as a person. It was an acute test of goodwill.

Anxious to gain the RSPB's total approval, great care was taken in outlining a plan for submission to HQ. Enthusiasm and idealism would weigh in my favour, but not at the expense of practicality. The cost of the project must be borne in mind, pains taken to point out the appeal of the new marshes to birdwatchers, visitor facilities provided. At present Balranald was an interesting but not very important reserve. With my sort of management, might its status not improve and thereby reflect credit on the society?

Two days of continuous paperwork, then up to the post office with a fat parcel for the RSPB. Returning to the caravan the marshes were there, on my left: Loch nam Feithean gleaming silverily under a fair but overcast sky, a fret of rush and reed against ruffled water, a flock of lapwings rising, crying and resettling. After several days of intense immersion in plans for the marshes, it seemed incredible that they should be unchanged, and I could no more populate that heart-fetching desolation with my voluntary conservation workers or dense packs of birds in artificial lagoons, than imagine it drained by Iain's mechanical shovel. The essence of the marsh was its watery horizontals, quiet under the sky. Would my plans turn it into a sort of outdoor zoo, spoil it as completely as any drainage? I had been elated, posting my parcel; now I felt uncertain and very alone.

Instead of going directly back to the caravan I left the road and walked around the head of the marshes. After a few hundred yards a weariness overcame me. Too much excitement, too much thinking, too little sleep during the last two nights. I waited for the feeling of weakness to pass, feeling strangely but not unpleasantly detached from my surroundings.

Not far away was an old straining post, once part of a fence which had bent or ended here, but now the rest of the fence had gone and only the old post remained, trailing a few strands of barbed wire. The wire was as old as the post; it wouldn't tear flesh like new barbed wire, but crumble into a palmful of rusty dust. Round its base grass grew almost as tall as the post, drooping seed heads with ears like barley, chaff-light, stirring in a wind so slight it left the loch waters unruffled.

A bird came to the post: a hen harrier, lifting silently as an owl out of the marsh. It was uneasy, wouldn't stay still; it rocked back and forth on top of the post, balancing with extensions of wings and long tail A female harrier and she was a beauty: plumage perfect in spite of the wear and tear of the breeding season, breast feathers reddish. Fierce, too-fiercely afraid, glaring at me, trying to focus me into something she could understand, hissing and snapping her beak. She launched off the post and flew low over the loch, above her own flying reflection, towards Goular church. I lost sight of her against the black mass of the building but a lapwing flock flew up again, flailing unco-ordinatedly about like bits of wind-caught newspaper. The last of the harrier was a silhouette, attenuated by hunting, against the western sky, then she dived down and was gone into the darkening body of the marshes.

From here one evening in April I had seen only harmony – marshes, birds, crofters, all equably interdependent – a traditional harmony, long lasting. Now, four months later, a derelict fence, a hunting harrier, distressed lapwings. Marshes quiet now and beautiful but a product of perpetual exploitation, birds and even plants competing for a niche, crofters pitching themselves against land, wetland and weather. Now me with my plans to exploit it all in the name of amenity.

Within a day or two a long letter came from the RSPB's reserve department at Sandy, expressing dismay at the drainage proposal and encouraging me to continue with attempts to secure management of the marshes. Approval was welcome, but the letter did strike a cautionary note in its last paragraphs. Marsh drainage or none, Balranald would still be a valuable reserve and in any negotia-

217

tions with the crofters I was therefore to avoid scrupulously any estrangement which might make the situation difficult for future wardens. The society would welcome the opportunity to manage the marshland, though the procedure might not be precisely as envisaged. Costs and labour had to be considered, the research department would have to do vegetational and topographical surveys to assess the consequences of excavation before lagoons could be opened. There was already a standard method of wetland management, established through experiment on similar habitats in the south, and my plans might have to be modified somewhat to fit in with overall reserve policy and budgeting.

Self-esteem took a healthy set-back on learning that my plans for management weren't so marvellously original after all. But the tone of moderation was in accord with my own subsequent reservations about changing the marshes too radically, spoiling their essential character with over-population and insensitive alteration of the scene. Perhaps the reserve's department had a greater regard for the aesthetics of conservation than I gave them credit for. On the whole the society's response was heartening, and with less than a fortnight of my season left, I felt an urgency to have the crofters' reactions to my suggestions. The letter from Sandy reminded me that at the end of the month I was scheduled to report at HQ in person and be briefed for my next location. This wasn't yet decided, but it was imperative to leave on time and to first complete my discussions over future developments with the crofters.

There would be no immediate decision from any of the three clerks of the relevant townships. They would have to consult all the other crofters and I quailed at the thought of it; a unanimous agreement from more than fifty of the most notoriously intractable people in Britain must be obtained before plans could go ahead.

At first all went propitiously. I talked to Lachie Fergusson of Balranald while he was digging potatoes and he was positively enthusiastic. Just imagine, all those wee birds. (And all those birdwatching tenants to his caravan, I caustically thought.) He intimated that no one in Balranald township would disagree – he, Lachie would see to it.

Murdo Macdonald at The Glebe had been elected township clerk for Hougharry only a few weeks before. Iain was present when I explained my scheme and both he and his father were disappointingly suspicious. Iain was quite sardonic.

'So that's what you've been up to since the birds stopped nesting. Thinking about holes and how to get more people here to put money in yon daft little tin at your door. And I thought to make a crofter, and a shooting man, out of you.'

It wasn't until Iain asked, 'Tell me, will it be you as warden here, next summer?' that the true cause of his resistance was revealed. He wasn't prepared to commit himself in agreement when next year's warden, the person who would carry out the work, might be a total stranger and someone with whom he had no affinity at all. I answered truthfully. 'I don't know, Iain. It's quite possible that I'll be sent back, and more likely if the plans go ahead. But I can't say for sure.' Iain was mollified.

'I hope it's all right,' he retracted. 'I don't really want to drive that digger into the marsh.' He turned to Murdo who as yet had made no comment. 'We'll see what we can do, but mind you, there's folk in Hougharry would say no just for the sake of disagreement. They'd argue over the offer of dry harvest weather, some of them.' It seemed that I could count on Iain's support, but no one else in Hougharry, not even Murdo.

The third and remaining township was Tigharry, a mile north of Hougharry, and its township clerk was a man called Angus Maclellan. He was a poet, a Gaelic bard, and he lived alone in a house on a hilltop. I plodded up there on an afternoon promising rain, with wind tugging at maps rolled under my arm. As befits a poet, Angus was a romantic, but he was also perspicacious. We pored over the maps until he was completely assured that he understood every aspect of the plans. His sharp mind probed my diagrams and pronouncements, testing for any possible disadvantage to the township. We talked for three hours and I couldn't doubt his sincerity or his ability to understand all the implications. If Angus gave a judgement it would be thoroughly considered and final. So at the end of our grilling session it was gratifying to hear him say: 'I canna see anything against it myself, and I'll put it to the township. But don't be too hopeful. I can't guarantee they'll all agree.'

Cottage renovations complete, paperwork finished and with ten days of the season still to run, I might have enjoyed a final period of

Orache growing amongst the dried kelp on the strandline in Vallay Sound

relaxation, but the tension of waiting for the crofters' verdict was unbearable. Because it now seemed so threatened and precious, I couldn't spend my time on the reserve, strolling around, accumulating memories which might trouble me in exile. Now was the time to explore those parts of Uist neglected through preoccupation with the reserve.

The long sand-dune peninsula of Baleshare attracted me. I drove at daybreak over the causeway, sand-flats paling with coming daylight, through ragged settlements where only the wind seemed awake, flapping washing left out all night, blowing hens through iris beds in patches of rough field which served as gardens. Cattle grouped against cottage walls, sheep lay like unwashed mats in doorways. There were no people about but the dogs were awake. Unkempt scrawny collies, all teeth and wild hair, rushing from open byres at the van, driving it into the next dog's territory by snapping at mudguards and tyres.

The crofts became fewer, the land opened out to a flat, low-lying moor. There, parked on the skyline, were three large open-backed lorries. All were long abandoned, windscreens smashed, no tyres on the rusting wheels, grass sprouting from the tailboards. They stood in line, playthings for wind and bored township children. A track ran on westward across a desolation of damp machair pastures. Dead flat, of dark salt-resistant turf, and fences everywhere although there was nothing in the fields except rabbits and hopping, scavenging crows. The track came to an end on a beach. On foot I followed the sands at the edge of tidal flats which stretched unbroken for 4 miles to the low coast of Benbecula. What a place for horizontals. My eyes ached for something tall against all that sky, my legs needed something to climb. I went on, wandering through salt-marshes where sea asters and thrift were withered brown but intact and set against green turf like some pressed and preserved floral decoration.

Towards the tip of the peninsula I came to sand-dunes and clambered gratefully up and down, imagining crests of marram 20ft above the sea to be ranges of mountains. I scaled Alps, Andes and Himalayas of white sand and came to a stop on a veritable sand-dune Everest, a huge isolated dune rising from grass through marram to a wind-shaped sandy peak. From the top stretched all the west coast of Baleshare, 5 miles of continuous beach, backed by dunes and facing the Atlantic.

For anything at all vertical I had to look due east, across the croftlands of Baleshare and the sandy west coast of North Uist, then across Uist's central moors to find at last a hill: Eaval, rugged axeshape with blade raised, cleaving north.

Seals followed me along the sea's edge, migrating terns hovered over me in the dunes, waders littered the bays and three whooper swans, first wild swans of the winter, swam in a loch among inland marshes. The levels were so vast and unremitting that they could seem hateful. But one day among mainland hills and woods I'd long for it; all of Baleshare, even its squalid dog-infested townships.

One day I glimpsed a paradise, the little green islands of the Sound of Harris, sand-fringed and set just like precious stones in the Sound, sunlit against a dark backcloth of Harris mountains. Another day brought me to coves and seacliffs like a fragment of Cornwall, where a farmhouse sat between green marsh and a white beach and almost looked picturesque. But wild geese over the sea and golden plovers mourning on the headlands, they were North Uist, never Wessex.

Several days poking about in the moors, reliving spring expeditions with Patricia, and then one day, just because it was so foul and windy, I climbed Eaval. At an old eagle's eyrie, I thought sadly and angrily of the poor breeding success of the Uist eagles. Only two eaglets fledged from seven pairs, and those two would be lucky to survive with crofters willing to trap them or poison them or to shoot them before they could properly fly.

Deer crossed the flank of Eaval and from its top a sudden temporary clearance gave a glimpse of mainland mountains. Leaves of a little wind-whipped rowan were browning with autumn and even on so small a tree swung a bunch of berries, vividly red. Red rowan berries, mountains which would soon have snow on them. I had a sudden fierce longing for the glens of Inverness and home.

Too long without a break, perhaps, from what was really an alien landscape, I decided not to go out early the morning after climbing Eaval, and was sitting in the caravan in disaffected mood when the Macdonalds' car drew up outside and Iain came to the door.

He had come to tell me that all three of the crofting townships had turned down my plan for managing the marshes. He had been asked to inform me of the decision, also to convey the regrets of all concerned, and to assure me that no one had anything against me personally. The reason for the refusal was that the crofters feared loss of control of the land to a body whose interests might not coincide with their own. Drainage, or the deepening, cleaning and widening of existing channels would proceed as planned, beginning in early winter.

Iain himself was deeply apologetic. He wanted me to know that the three township clerks – his father at Hougharry, Lachie at Balranald and Angus at Tigharry – had all spoken in my favour, but the body of opinion was against the scheme. Who, after all, could blame the crofters? Why should they pass lands which had been grazed by their animals for generations into the hands of a comparative stranger, working for a remote authority, all to a purpose which conflicted with traditional ideas of how land should be used?

I had to agree with Iain. It was expecting too much. It was futile to rage against the crofters, but gratifying to know that those with whom I did have acquaintance had all supported the scheme. Big affable Lachie, poet Angus, Murdo and Iain himself, true friends at The Glebe. The others couldn't be accused of lack of magnanimity; nowhere else in Britain could any body of landowners even be approached with a plan like mine.

Iain was saying something about drainage. It mightn't affect the marshes and birds so seriously as feared. It had been done before and the marshes survived. He might come to some arrangement with the RSPB about a sluice set at the outlet from Loch nam Feithean. He could do this independently of the other crofters since that part of the drainage system was on Glebe land.

I thanked him for his support, for this latest suggestion. Yes, we would discuss it tomorrow. Meanwhile, I'd like to be left to think about things, alone.

Iain understandingly went, saying he'd call again next morning.

As soon as he had gone, I took my binoculars and stick and followed him up the track to The Glebe, turning off to walk across the end of the marshes. I felt astonishingly light-hearted, in contrast to the depression of the last few days and this morning before Iain had brought his news.

Unable to bear the sight of the marshes for a week, I could look at them again now. They'd be drained or they wouldn't be drained, it was out of my hands. And there might be something left; some of Loch nam Feithean, a patch of rushes here and there, some iris for the corncrakes to skulk about in. No lagoons, no birdwatchers' hides, but I was secretly relieved to be free of any conflict between a small quiet marshland and a larger one developed for amenity.

No lagoons, but the wind would blow in the rushes, it would ruffle the shaggy coats of the islanders' cattle as they grazed in the

Curlew

attractive, apparently unspoiled damp hollow. I examined the outlet from Loch nam Feithean where Iain had so generously suggested installing a sluice, eyed the comparative levels of marsh, loch, ditch and field. Yes, perhaps something could be done. Half a dozen teal slanted down to splash land nearby. There would always be a place here, surely, for half a dozen teal.

Soon, happily past the reed-beds and Balranald House, I'd call and see Patricia later, on my way back. More marsh and salt-marsh to the edge of Loch Paible. Paible wasn't threatened by drainage. How appealing it was, sand-flats and mud-flats seamed by creeks at ebb-tide of a fair September morning.

I sat at the edge of the salt-marsh where it gave way to estuarine sand, my backside on sodden turf and feet on a shelf of seaweed left to rot there by the last tide. Near me a fence went out across the sands so far, and ended. The wires were broken, the fence was useless except as a place for gulls to perch or for the tide to hang more seaweed to dry. Waders flicked by, a cow was standing in a creek chewing a thick stem of kelp. She shouldn't be there at this time, the cow, she had wandered unnoticed from some ill-fenced field in the Paible croftlands. I felt a surge of affection for Paible; only a small tidal inlet, but conveying more of essential Uist than anywhere else on the island.

A curlew walked out and stood at the side of a creek. It looked round, didn't see me, called once and began to feed. I could come to Paible any time and feel myself in touch with the island's character and its curlews. Any time – but in three days I would be leaving. I had been anxious to leave, to be back in a wooded landscape while the leaves held autumn colour, and see my family, the landscape of home. But Uist would draw me again after a few days on the mainland. At RSPB headquarters at the end of the month I'd certainly request to be sent back, to warden the reserve next season, see the effects of drainage on the marsh and supervise the positioning of Iain's sluice.

There were features of Uist for which I had developed a special affinity. The people: the Glebe Macdonalds, Patricia, Cameron. The landscape of desolate watery moorlands, the many birds; and most keenly I'd miss this view across salt-marsh and estuarine sands to the croftlands of Paible, with a curlew in the foreground.

I got to my feet then, calculating what remained for me to do during the last few days of my season. Thank the crofters for considering my schemes, inform the RSPB of their final decision and complete paperwork. Say farewell to people and places and do my packing.

Meanwhile, it would be enough to dawdle what remained of the afternoon away down the ebb-tide flats of Paible to its mouth, walk up Scolpaig strand with evening light on sand and sea and come back over the gloaming machair to Balranald House. It would be late before I had finished talking to Patricia, very dark for walking home. But I'd get direction from Cameron's light at Goular and the lights of Hougharry township reflecting in the waters of the marsh.

Curlew

ACKNOWLEDGEMENTS

The author's widow and the publishers would like to thank the following for their help in providing photographs for this book: the RSPB (page 6); John Macleod (pages 18, 34, 80, 93, 126, 147, 188, 194, 195, 198 and 208); the Scottish Tourist Board (pages 20, 75 and 136); Julian Cremona Photographic (pages 23, 38, 54, 114 and 220); and Mrs E. Arthur for her husband's colour photograph of the corncrake on page 51.